OVERCOMING EXECUTIVE
MID-LIFE CRISIS

OVERCOMING EXECUTIVE
MID-LIFE CRISIS

HOMER R. FIGLER

A WILEY—INTERSCIENCE PUBLICATION
John Wiley & Sons • New York • Chichester • Brisbane • Toronto

Library of Congress Cataloging in Publication Data:

Figler, Homer R   1923-
  Overcoming executive mid-life crisis.

  "A Wiley-Interscience publication."
  Includes index.
    1. Executives.   2.   Middle age.   3.   Age and
employment.   I.   Title.

HF5500.2.F52   \658.4′07′14   77-29206
ISBN 0-471-04147-5

Printed in the United States of America

10 9 8 7 6 5 4 3 2 1

This book is dedicated to—
My helper . . .
My wife . . .
Arlene

Preface

Middle age is a transition. For most people, it is viewed as a dreadful period of slowing down, a period that will end in a catastrophy—old age—that can be avoided by being denied. For some others, it is a period of peak achievement, the fruition of training and experience in the accomplishment of long-sought-after goals, a period that will come to an end in retirement, a condition again viewed without joy or hope. For a few people—far too few—it is one part of a continuous whole, every segment of which is as exciting, productive and joy filled as is every other.

This book has been written for those in the first two categories who want to be part of the third group. I began writing this book for executives because my work has been with that group for so many years. As the book developed, however, I found that the basic principles apply to everyone. Thus this book is intended for all people.

Statistics, as inadequate as they may be, point to a disproportionate number of people—middle-aged people—as making a disproportionate number of bad decisions. The decisions and the motives underlying them show clearly that a great many middle-agers are unhappy and that at some time during mid-life they reach a critical point at which they are impelled to action—much too often with negative consequences. This critical point has been termed the Mid-Life Crisis.

An increasing amount has been written in recent years about the so-called Mid-Life Crisis. Very little of this can be applied directly, *by the individual,* into his own life. This book has been written both for the person who is experiencing mid-life problems and for those who wish to avoid them in the first place.

Every person who has ever lived is a unique being whose development, growth, and personality are the end result of a combination of his heredity and all of the things that have happened since birth. No one is "average." On the other hand, everyone faces certain common traumatic events such as aging, illness, retirement, death, loss of friends, and so on. The impact on the individual of these events and the way in which he reacts to them depend very much on the extent to which the individual is prepared to deal with the event and even his understanding of it.

I have lived most of my life since college graduation in the world of the corporate executive. During those years I have spoken with and/or interviewed in depth thousands of executives at all levels, in all kinds of businesses and organizations, ranging from small to huge. One fact has emerged and has been polished into crystal clarity: on the job, the executive is the decision maker—the planner—the organizer—the leader—BUT all of those roles are played and all of those actions are taken by a person—a human being. As such, he faces all of the trauma, all of the pain, all of the joys and, despite his power and influence over others, reacts in the same way as does every other human being to all the facts of life.

This book has been written for anyone who is interested in learning how to deal with the normal trauma of life (particularly as embodied in the so-called Mid-Life Crisis), to avoid or overcome the problems associated with aging, and to live a happier life as a result. (Is this book for women? The last time I looked, they were people too, and it is for people!)

No magic potions or instant cures are offered. There are no gimmicks, and there is nothing to buy. If, however, you follow the instructions given in this book, have the determination

PREFACE ix

to make the necessary effort, and really want a better life, you can have it.

This book was a long time in production. The research, including interviews with several thousand people, took place over a number of years. The book itself was written over a 3-year period, and there were times when its completion seemed doubtful. Throughout, four people were unstinting in their encouragement and help: first, my wife, to whom this book is dedicated; next, Arthur P. (Bart) Bartholomew, Jr., whose support was constant and unwavering; and George Tasso, about whom I can truly say, no man has ever had a better friend. These three and Lisa Roberto, who typed and critiqued the manuscript, have my deepest appreciation. In a very real way, without their help it probably would not have happened.

Hastings-on-Hudson, New York   Homer R. Figler
December, 1977

Special Notes

• The Mid-Life Crisis is a real, existing phenomenon. The examples cited for illustrative purposes are also of real people. In every case, however, without exception, identification, even by the person or persons involved, is impossible. Essential statistical data—job fields, types of industry, job titles, and the like—have all been disguised. The purpose of an illustrative case is to clarify a point. The ability to identify the person would only add confusion.

• Throughout this book, masculine pronouns are used simply to avoid awkward phraseology and difficult sentence construction. The reader can assume that "his" means "his or hers," for the principles involved apply to women just as much as they do to men.

• Because every human being is unique, each reader will see himself in different things that are said in this book. If a sensitive nerve is touched, it may be difficult for you to retain perspective. Accordingly, I have incorporated a great deal of redundancy into the book, just as there would be if I were speaking to someone face-to-face, individually, or even with a large group. If redundancy bothers you, I apologize for it, but I will not eliminate the repetition, because I believe that it may help someone in crystallizing a heretofore amorphous problem. I firmly believe that affirmative action provides hope in any human problem, and throughout I note that fact, especially when talking about the more negative consequences of inaction.

• Throughout this book I make reference to both child–parent conflict and to the destructive behavior of some young people. This is not intended as a "put-down" for the younger generation. Indeed, I have great faith in the youth of our nation. But, in this book I am concerned with two specific groups of people—those who are middle-aged and those who recognize that one day they will be middle-aged. Specifically, I am interested in the problems they face and the causes and solutions to those problems. The behavior of all young people in general and some few extremists are a contributing cause to the problems of many middle-agers. Here I merely *report* with respect to the majority. Where you detect criticism—it is mainly for those in the extreme group.

H.R.F.

Contents

OVERCOMING EXECUTIVE
MID-LIFE CRISIS

1 Introduction to the Problem

Because you are reading this, the chances are very good that you are either middle-aged or will enter those middle years in the not-too-distant future.

It is also more than likely that you know someone personally who has already experienced or is now going through an experience that is a direct result of being middle-aged. And, the odds are that the experience was or is negative:

- A couple in their mid-40s, after 20 years of marriage and with three teenage children, file for divorce.
- A marketing vice president becomes noticeable by the amount of time he spends at home with trivial physical ailments.
- A department head is seen outside of work in the company of his secretary often enough to raise comment.
- A plant manager, whose career can only be described as successful, walks into corporate headquarters and resigns. Even though he has risen through the ranks—on a fast track—and is regarded as "a comer" for the future, he states that he feels that his future is limited in the company and thus he wants "out."
- One of the best foremen in the plant, who for years has always arrived early and stayed late, gradually begins working only from 9:00 to 5:00, develops a negative attitude, and earns a reputation as a "complainer."
- The head of a large engineering group has several drinks for lunch, rarely eats the food he orders, and is noticed going into a nearby bar at coffee-break time.

• At the annual company picnic, a few people who know them well notice that the Personnel Manager and his wife spend no time together and rarely even speak to each other.

• A plant superintendent becomes excessively demanding of his young executives and begins driving himself just as hard.

• A very successful salesman, whom everyone believes to have a sound family life, begins "making a play" for every young girl he meets.

All these people have one thing in common. Something has changed in their outlook on life, and that change has had a substantial impact on their behavior. Without exception, the change has been negative, and in most cases the end result has been a disaster—minor or major. This traumatic and dramatic change in one's outlook on life, that has such a disruptive effect in so many cases, has only recently become a subject of serious study. It is called the Mid-Life Crisis.

MID-LIFE CRISIS—DEFINED

The Mid-Life Crisis is nothing more nor less than a problem brought about by the aging process—a problem that is aggravated by an interaction of the person's personality and the world in which he lives. It is essential to understand that there is nothing unique or different about growing older today than has been true in the past. On the other hand, the attitudes toward aging have shifted, and the setting in which the process is occurring has become very complex.

The interaction between social attitudes and the environmental setting in which we live today impinge on what is a fairly normal phenomenon. The end result is a crisis in too many cases.

In one sense "crisis" is a very strong word. As you grow, your perspective changes. It is common to hear middle agers say, "You see things differently than you did when you were younger." The resultant change that occurs is usually a product of:

1. Your own personality makeup.
2. Your outlook on life.
3. Your personal environment—psychological, social, and physical.

The effect of the change in perspective can be major or minor. It can be transitory or permanent. It can involve and impact others, or be confined to you alone.

Thus the term Mid-Life Crisis conjures up a vision of something massive that occurs suddenly in middle age. Fortunately or unfortunately, it is not that simple. The facts are:

  • *Age at Onset:* People are so different one from the other that the types of problems associated with the so-called Mid-Life Crisis can occur in someone who is relatively young or can be first seen at what most people would consider an advanced age. In this context the association between the terms *mid-life* and *middle-aged* is unfortunate. The erroneous inference is that the "good" half of life is over and that the "bad" half has begun.
  • *Rate of Onset:* Some of the symptoms of the Mid-Life Crisis are present at several points in one's life but take on added significance in the middle years, where they occur in combination with other events that accent their occurrence. The matter of individual differences is primary. For some people the symptoms occur seemingly overnight, and with others the onset is so gradual as to be unnoticed until pointed out by someone else or otherwise brought to the victim's attention.
  • *Scope of Occurrence:* The problem here is to define the extent or nature of a "crisis." Symptoms, when they occur, can be exceedingly mild or extremely severe. Accordingly, it is commonplace for some people to experience a minor discomfort that is eventually overcome, whereas other people are led to the point of drastic action, even as drastic as suicide in some extreme cases.

All the foregoing factors suggest a variability which makes the Mid-Life Crisis a very elusive concept that is difficult to pin down. This is true. In the final analysis, it cannot be thought of as a generalized kind of thing to be approached on the basis of "mass-production" intervention. Each person's case must be dealt with individually. But, when that approach is taken, the end result can be highly productive and beneficial.

To the person experiencing a Mid-Life Crisis—of almost any severity level—the problem looks huge and possibly even insurmountable. I can promise you that there is hope and help for overcoming the problem and for happiness. Many of even the darkest problems disappear with only a modest amount of effort. There is a price, however! (Nothing in this life is free.) You must *work* for a solution, but in this case, I think you will find that even the work involved can be enjoyable.

AGE—AGE—AGE—AGE—AGE

If the word *age* and all the concepts related to it could be eliminated from our dictionary and language, the Mid-Life Crisis and many other of man's problems would disappear.

Whenever the topic of the Mid-Life Crisis comes up, the first question that is asked—invariably—is, "At what age does it occur?".

Because people are so insistent on wanting to know when "middle age" is, I usually give an answer like, "between the ages of 35 and 55." Those numbers, however, are meaningless!

The aging process is so variable from one person to the next—it is so dependent on both psychological and physiological factors—and the concept is so emotional—that the entire problem almost defies description.

There is no question in my mind that a major cause of the Mid-Life Crisis is a simple conditioned response to the concept of age.

Before he is able to talk, an infant is bombarded with commands and demands that he gauge his behavior *and his thinking* in terms of his chronological age—irrespective of even common-sense evidence to the contrary. From the very earliest days of his conscious awareness of such relationships, the child is taught that his chronological age dictates what he can and cannot do in most of his social relationships, what his status and qualifications are legally, and (unfortunately) how he should think, act, and feel about himself—facts to the contrary notwithstanding. As a very young boy, the child is told:

- "You are too old to act like that."
- "You are not old enough yet to do things like that."
- "Big boys don't do that."
- "You have to go to school because you are 6 years old, that's why!"
- "Today you are a man."

This close tie between behavior and age is continued with legal enforcement. As the youngster grows, he gains legal status, including both privileges and responsibilities:

- At a certain age, usually 15 or 16, he can get working papers.
- Drivers' licenses are granted at various levels and at various ages.
- At age 18, a young person assumes many legal rights and responsibilities.
- At age 21, a young person becomes totally, legally free.

Along the way to adolescence there are social and religious ceremonies that mark points of achievement that are strictly related to age, irrespective of psychological, social, or physical development. In many churches, young people are given adult status in the congregation mainly on the basis of chronological age, with total disregard for their psychological, intellectual, or social readiness for such status. Woe betide the pastor or rabbi who has the temerity to suggest that Johnny isn't ready. Of equally lamentable proportions, the same concept has entered our public educational system. In far too many cases "passing" is determined more by a misguided concern for social development than proper attention to the child's intellectual readiness for moving on to the next level. The same parent who voted for school board members who promise more emphasis on "culture" and less on old-fashioned things like basic reading, writing, and arithmetic (and grades) will cry loudly about the poor treatment Johnnie receives when he is denied the job he wants because he can't read or write.

This whole concept of age is closely related to that of "grouping" (Chapter 4) and is a potent force in dictating many people's actions. For example, in recent years reaching the age of 30 has become a critical point. For many adolescents, those who are over 30 are "the enemy" who represent the establishment and whose hypocrisy must be defeated by the purity of the younger generation's ideals. "Age 30" or "old goat of 40" parties are quite common—the concept here being that, at that point in a person's life, they are ready for the scrap heap.

By the time middle age comes along, the individual is so conditioned that he does not bother to stop and think about what he should do. Even though he may be in the best physical condition of his entire life, be fully mentally alert and highly creative, have great amounts of physical energy and strength, and be as sexually active as ever, he "knows" that none of these things *should* be. Accordingly, he "thinks himself" into mental and physical deterioration and begins that long process which eventually ends in senility and/or old age—long before either needs to be.

A great deal of research is needed in this area, but on the basis of my own professional experience and observations, I have no doubts whatsoever that the process of mental and physical deterioration can be slowed remarkably, into very advanced ages.

The secret in this process is to avoid thinking of yourself in terms of chronological age. Instead, look at yourself as you are today—totally ignore your age as a factor in thinking about what you are, who you are, and what you are able to do.

For example, I know that I cannot do a lot of things—physically—that I was able to do 25 years ago. However, I do not dwell on that with regret, for those abilities were pertinent to that time and that time is gone. Today I am able to do what I am able to do now. The kinds of skills, abilities, knowledge, and potentials I have today are different than they were 25 years ago, but also they are far greater in number, and in many ways they are better.

SYMPTOMS OF THE MID-LIFE CRISIS

The symptoms of the Mid-Life Crisis are many and varied. (A later chapter is devoted entirely to this topic.) Undergirding and overshadowing them all is either active unhappiness or, at the very least, a lack of happiness.

Although increasing numbers of people are experiencing extreme symptoms (results), the most common problem is that of simply living out an unhappy life.

The toll in the business world is hidden more often than not, but once again the cost is growing and is already excessive. We have known for many many years that a person's personal life affects his job performance and vice versa. Thus it should be no surprise to find out that when an executive is having trouble at home or is personally unhappy, his productivity on the job suffers. When he makes a mistake or a wrong decision, the result is usually visible. Often, however, he errs by avoiding a difficult decision, taking the "safe way" out, or he fails to pick up on an opportunity that involves some risk but of which no one else is aware. In these ways, the organization suffers, perhaps not by a direct loss but by profits that could have been there had he been performing his job as he should have.

CAUSES OF THE MID-LIFE CRISIS

The Mid-Life Crisis is caused by an interaction of normal human events and the society in which we live. In a sense it is the result of a lack of planning, for, almost without exception, most of life's "normal" problems can be avoided if only the person would look ahead and plan to avoid the problem in the first place.

Possibly one of the best examples of the interaction of society and personal causes as affected by a lack of planning can be seen in our current divorce rate. In the old days (one generation ago!) it was a disgrace to be divorced. There was major social pressure brought to bear on a couple who were experiencing difficulty, and they were forced to stay together whether they wanted to or not. In some cases, this led to a marriage filled with a lifetime of unhappiness; faced with the mandatory requirement of staying together, however, many couples also managed to work out their problems and actually lived "very happily ever after."

Today, the social pressure against divorce is almost gone. When a young couple marries, they are not truly in love (since love must grow over a period of time and be based on many shared experiences). The early years can be predicted with great accuracy to have many problems as the two learn to adjust to each other and to living together in a family relationship. Many couples who successfully get through those years do so because they do some planning in ways and means of handling conflict, as well as exercise common sense when problems crop up.

The Mid-Life Crisis is composed of such common occurrences. It, too, can be avoided, or if it occurs, it can be resolved successfully.

LIFE'S PREDICTABLES

One of man's greatest weaknesses and handicaps is his ability to avoid doing what is good for himself. In a very real sense, man has an infinite capacity to grow, develop, and discover. He also has an undreamed of and incalculable capacity to create problems for himself.

One of man's delusions that gets him into constant trouble is the fantasy that he will continue on into the future exactly as he is today. Why, then, is it necessary to be concerned about such things as a Mid-Life Crisis or events beyond that point? The answer is that there are only three things in life that can be predicted with accuracy:

1. *You will change continuously from birth onward:* You come into this world with certain basic attributes, talents, abilities, and characteristics. As you grow, these are developed and modified by your experiences, and you *today* are the end result of the interaction of what you start with and what happens to you. Throughout your life that interaction continues (the physical and psychological characteristics on the one side and the things you experience and those that happen to you on the other), all within the influencing framework of the world in which you live.

2. *Your world will continuously change:* The world you live in influences every aspect of your life. It can be warm and friendly, threatening and grim, physically or psychologically harmful, anxiety producing, and so on. Whatever it is, it will change. You are affected by the world in which you live, and what you are at any one point in time is the result of the interaction of it with your changing self.

3. *At the end of each person's life is death:* As one is born, it is predictable that so too one must die. (This point is dealt with in much greater detail later on in Chapter 4.)

It should be noted that the Mid-Life Crisis is not listed as one of the three predictables. It is not necessary for you to experience an age-related crisis in your life, and, in fact, to avoid it is rather simple.

The cost in pain, suffering, and dollars that can be saved by just a little planning is unbelievable.

HOW TO AVOID HAVING A MID-LIFE CRISIS

The process involved in avoiding or even of getting rid of a Mid-Life Crisis is quite simple. Making it happen, however, is again something else. The steps are as follows:

1. You must understand what is going on.
2. You must know who you are (understand yourself). The average person has not ever taken the time or been sufficiently honest with himself to really know who he is.
3. You must know what to do (plan).
4. You must be willing to make the necessary effort (commitment).

Items 1, 2, and 3 are fairly easy to accomplish. The commitment can be very difficult, and it is in this area that most failures occur.

I would be less than honest if I were not to say that some of the steps required involve a great deal of hard work. Indeed, to achieve all the happiness that should be yours, you will have to become directly involved in charting the path of your own destiny instead of merely letting yourself be pushed around by events and circumstances.

On the other hand, most of the people I have worked with professionally would like to be happier than they are and be more in charge of their own lives. The problem usually is that they do not know how to begin or to proceed. This book is dedicated to those two tasks.

2 The Setting

The basic ingredients of the Mid-Life Crisis—and the plain problems of aging that do not qualify for crisis status—are essentially normal events. In a very real sense, these events have been occurring to man for a very long time, without the profound effect that appears to be the case today, or where there have been problems the intensity and severity thereof have never been so great.

Why is today different from the past, even the recent past?

I am sure that this question has been asked by everyone of his or her own time, but I believe that today *is* different, primarily because of the technological advances that have occurred in the past few years.

In most points of history, there has been a fairly well-defined connection between the past and the future. Of greatest importance, the future has had some degree of predictability, in general if not in the specific, and the present has had a comprehensible order. This is no longer true. The end result for the individual is difficult to assess, yet surely the pressures created by these problems are having an impact on every facet of our lives, and most particularly this is true in relation to antagonizing the already visible stresses of the middle years.

Any attempt to explain infinitely complex matters must always be incomplete. For our purposes, such detail is not required. It will serve our purposes to outline the situation in general terms, with just enough detail to indicate how the world in which we live has an impact on us and our behavior.

YESTERDAY

The world in which most middle-agers grew up was

1. *Relatively Stable:* Change occurred, as it always has, but as new things came along there was time to understand them, time to assess the impact they had on our lives, and time to become comfortable and accustomed to them before the next change occurred.

2. *Guided by Generally Shared Values:* Without making any attempt to defend the quality of the value systems in existence, social injustice, or civil rights (one generation ago), most people had similar values, there was a generally agreed upon difference between right and wrong based on a common standard, and it was acceptable to be patriotic.

3. *Well Defined in Form and Shape:* We were protected from foreign invasion and danger by two oceans, our government was stable, we thought of ourselves as being the finest nation on the face of the earth, and our total environment had dignity and purpose.

THE SETTING FOR THE MID-LIFE CRISIS

Today, the world described above no longer exists. We are living in a time of change—change that is occurring at such a rapid pace we have lost our ability to, individually, adapt to that change.

In a very real sense, what we are seeing constitutes a revolution—a revolution that is only in a minor way industrial. In a much more significant way it is technological, political, social and behavioral in character. Our society is composed of many forces operating in many directions, and it is becoming increasingly difficult for the average individual to "cope" with what he sees going on around him.

1. Technology and Cultural Lag. The pace of technological change in the past few years has been such that there is no way man can hope to incorporate the consequences of each achievement into his life or even general consciousness. (The psychological factor of "consequences" is of extreme importance here.) I do not deny that man has made technological advances from the time of the caveman to the present. However, the technology of the past 50 years has, to a far greater extent than ever before, had a direct impact on the individual, and this is a significant change from prior times. For example, the invention of the internal combustion engine was a boon to mankind, and over a period of 100 years has proven to be both a blessing and a curse. Upon its introduction, and for long afterward, there was no generally recognized "consequence." On the other hand, the development of the atomic bomb became an immediate threat to the existence of every human being on the day of its creation and the awareness of this (consequence) quickly became immediate, personal, and worldwide. We are also all aware of the fact that these devices are held by countries and individuals who are potentially capable of using them, even though it might mean their own destruction as well as ours. I believe firmly that the entire younger generation has been affected by this Damoclean sword and that the Mid-Life Crisis is also a consequence in part.

2. Communication Overload. We have become so blasé about cataclysmic changes in the world that we have difficulty comprehending the true impact of those events that occur in seemingly endless progression. For example, as young as I was at the time, I can remember clearly the extended news coverage and celebration of Lindbergh's crossing of the Atlantic. When we successfully landed a space vehicle/research laboratory on the planet Mars, many newspapers treated this as a subheadline item, and a few even relegated it to something other than page 1.

The reasons for our attitudes are many and varied. One is that we have become "numb" to the rapid succession of truly remarkable achievements of man's inventive genius and are simply unable to comprehend the full impact of one before another comes along to take its place. In addition, today we are innundated with so much information we simply cannot understand the true meaning of it all. Also, most people depend on 5-minute radio broadcasts and 30-minute television newscasts for the news. From these sources they get only "headlines," rarely the whole story; thus meaning, consequence, and even wholeness are lost.

The vast array of sources of information is so imposing that it leads to confusion, and the realization of lack of knowledge can lead to insecurity. To *know* today requires effort, and too few people are willing to make that effort.

3. Social Upheaval. Social upheaval is not new. Today, it only adds to the other conditions and makes them worse. What is new is that facet of social upheaval that can be attributed to social mobility—both geographic and in terms of a rapid change in the order of society.

For all the years of man's existence, the social structure of the world has been based on white male domination. In less than a single generation, all that has changed, as well it should, but the rate of change has permitted no opportunity for comfortable incorporation and transition into the mental processes of the average person. Thus it sits as an uncomfortably unassimilated and dangerous problem.

The complexity of today's social upheaval should not be underestimated, no more than should its effects. In a later chapter, I speak about parent-child conflict and the role that it plays in the Mid-Life Crisis, but it must also be mentioned here, for it is also part of the setting.

Peer pressure has given most teenagers the strength necessary to reject their parents' values and create conflict thereby between themselves and their parents, but also within the minds of the parents alone. For example, many parents fail in

their attempts to get their children to see the long-term consequences of the use of alcohol, LSD, marijuana, and the like.
That failure brings on a feeling of helplessness, and that feeling
serves as a major source of conflict. As reports showing increasing proof of the consequences of drug use (even to the point
of long-term biological damage) continue, the feelings of helplessness and conflict grow.

The picture becomes even more complicated when you
look at the attitudes of the two groups separately. Many young
people follow the philosophy that this is the "now generation."
In practice, this means that whatever one finds reason for doing now should be done, irrespective of the long-term consequences (a typical example of immaturity). Usually, there is
some pleasurable aspect to whatever it is that the youngster
wants to do now—certainly, there is a great deal of peer pressure involved.

With the parents, in addition to the feelings of helplessness, there is also a great deal of anxiety and, frequently, guilt
feelings. All too often, parents have the unfounded doubt that
they did everything they could to prevent the problem in the
first place, and thus self-recrimination gets all mixed up in the
other feelings as well. As is mentioned elsewhere in this book,
even this situation becomes almost indescribably complicated
under certain conditions. Two examples suit the purpose here
at this stage:

• In the midst of the doubt mentioned above, when the
child reaches adult status, it is quite possible for him or her
to accuse the parents of not having tried "hard enough" to
keep him or her from the negative action in the first place.
The parents may have tried every strategy in the book (given
preferential rewards to the misbehaving child over the other
children in the family, disrupted the lives of the rest of the
family, given up family activities because of the lack of consideration for anyone else by the self-centered child, and
even destroyed the normal atmosphere in the family with ar-
guments, once all else had failed) all to no avail. When ac-

cused of not having made sufficient effort, the parents' anxiety can turn to guilt, and self-doubt can build to neurotic
or even psychotic proportions.

• Some parents today complicate their own feelings by a
jealousy for the liberal lives their own children lead. These
parents grew up in a strict moral environment. That background causes them to reject the liberality of today's society,
while at the same time, an element of jealousy creeps in to
complicate the emotion—with the end result being one of
conflict.

4. Social Value Systems. Value systems are changing so rapidly that this problem alone is destroying many families and is
threatening the entire family structure of our society.

Also, to Mr. Average-Law-Abiding-Tax-Paying-Citizen, it
seems today as though everyone has rights except him.

a. He obeys the law, yet every day he sees evidence of others breaking the law with impunity. Drivers violate national
speed limits; draft dodgers are told to come home, that "all
is forgiven," while those who in obedience to the law
stepped forward in honor and provided them a country to
come back to are thus dishonored; thieves can bargain their
way out of jail terms; rapists and worse are freed to prey on
society again; and so on and so on and so on, endlessly.

b. There is an ever-lowering quality of goods and services.
In one brief week, recently, one person found:

• A purchase of three pairs of socks required two to be
returned as defective.
• A recently purchased new automobile had to be returned for the seventh time for the same repair.
• A new part on a sink faucet was defective and required
a second visit by the plumber.
• A new suit had to be returned for repairs when a seam
split on the first wearing.

c. It is proposed that illegal aliens, who have been successful in evading the law long enough, be made citizens and
forgiven their illegal entry.

d. Elected public officials steal, lie, and cheat, with at most,
a censure consisting of a soon-to-be-forgotten slap on the
wrist.

e. He grew up in a world where his family physician called on him at home when he was ill. Today he must go to the doctor's office no matter how ill he is and more often than not will find treatment focused on the physical problem with total disregard for the fact that there is a human being attached to the injured organ or part.

f. Immorality stretches from the highest levels of government and business to his next-door neighbor.

g. Hoodlums walk the street at will.

h. Industry pollutes and poisons his environment.

i. Discourtesy is so commonplace as to be the norm—even in the actions of children, whose behavior is supported by their parents.

Insulted, ripped off, cheated, and abused, his sensibilities are offended and his personal values are derided. He feels himself swept along by a tide of social degeneration he is powerless to do anything about or even cope with, in terms of his personal life as a member of his own society.

5. Loss of Religious Faith. This subject is far too vast to describe here. Suffice it to say that throughout history, where man has attempted to exist in society without belief in some supreme being that serves to regulate that society, the society has failed. This is no less true today.

With all the foregoing, ours is a time of paradox and conflict. We have, as daily companions: war and peace, fast-comprehensive communication (albeit we must reduce the reading level of college textbooks because our children are graduating almost illiterate from high school), advances in knowledge and technology undreamed of only a few years ago (while people in some parts of the world are starving), and the ability to prevent polio, smallpox, and other serious ailments (although we still cannot prevent or cure the common cold).

It is clear that man has an infinite capacity to grow, develop and discover. He also has an undreamed of and incalculable capacity to create problems for himself. We are living in a time of untold opportunity, yet large numbers of our population refuse to accept simple responsibility. This is an era of discovery and doubt; although people have been dying for millions of years, now we find suddenly that we do not know what death is or how to deal with it appropriately.

THE SETTING AND MID-LIFE PROBLEMS

The Mid-Life Crisis, for most people, is a period of unhappiness that never really reaches the catastrophic extremes that are possible. On the other hand, infidelity and divorce are growing and have become major problems for middle agers, and that is problem enough for almost anyone.

Most Mid-Life Crisis problems can be solved by the individual, him or herself, once they recognize the problem for what it is, dig into the facts, and have reassurance that they can deal with it on their own. It is surprising how many people to whom I have given guidance in this area have expressed a concern over whether or not they will need to see a psychiatrist. With reassurance that this will probably not be necessary (and if it is, it won't hurt) there is a visible reduction in tension.

As is noted later, a "normal" consequence of "normal" mid-life problems always involves some emotional upheaval. When this occurs in a social setting that is stable, well defined, and dependable, the individual can draw strength from his environment and very likely work his way through the problems without serious difficulty. On the other hand, if society itself is unstable, the individual is required to draw on his own inner resources. If these are weak or fragile and the problems he is experiencing are strong, he is in trouble. Today, it is a rare situation in which one can draw strength from the society in which he exists and, as is described later, most people's inner resources are weak or nonexistent.

Thus the problem!

3 Symptoms

(Causes?)

By this time, you should know that human behavior and its causes are exceedingly complex. Frequently, they do not follow any rules of logic or reason.

These statements are so true that for any rule which appears to apply to all people, you must always be prepared for exceptions, for there will be some. Moreover, what appears to be true concerning an individual at one point may be quite different at another time. In looking for reasons for behavior, you have to look both inside as well as outside of the person's mind. For example, a friend may receive a gift with obvious joy and shortly thereafter react with very little response in identical circumstances. The difference could be as simple as a difference in mood in the recipient, or it could be the result of something quite complex.

The main point of this discussion is that throughout this book, concepts such as symptoms and causes, to mention only two, are classified and discussed individually. It is *essential* to keep in mind that within the individual nothing occurs in isolation, everything is transitory, and yet throughout there are consistencies, even if they are at times hidden or obscured by momentary conditions.

Accordingly, the classification schemes used here are intended to permit discussion of the individual elements. But those elements should not be restricted or confined solely to the discussion of their definitions. The human organism is much too complex to be confined by such simple mechanisms.

SYMPTOMS OF THE MID-LIFE CRISIS

In keeping with the foregoing discussion and as expressed in the title of this chapter, it is very difficult to separate symptoms and causes when dealing with mid-life problems. The problem here is that what is at one time a symptom may well become a cause in the cyclical development of a problem. The purpose of classification is discussion and explanation. The ultimate and truly important point here is to recognize whether a symptom or a cause (whichever it is in your case) is present. Once recognized, the next step is not to worry about classifying it, but to determine the proper course of remedial action.

Further, the symptoms of the Mid-Life Crisis generally occur slowly and usually are not noticed until well developed. Many of the symptoms are simply aggravations or expansions of existing behaviors or personality traits, and they are thus difficult to detect as something new or different within the individual. Therein lies a major source of the problem of studying the crisis. The symptom may be a change from the typical behavior of the person because it is difficult, *or* it may be a change only in degree of the person's usual mode of behavior. For example:

  • *Different* behavior would be seen in the person who has always followed the company's rules and met all his responsibilities in a timely and satisfactory manner but who begins to miss deadlines, perform in a less-than-satisfactory way, show up late in the morning or go home early in the afternoon, begin taking time off for flimsy excuses, and so on.
  • *Change* as a degree of difference is exemplified by the executive who has always set high standards but now demands (literally) the impossible.

The Mid-Life Crisis is not a single event that can be isolated from the rest of a person's life. The person can experience symptoms in one, two, or more areas and in all degrees, combinations, and permutations. It is, therefore, almost impossible to separate the symptoms from their causes. It is also almost impossible to draw any common lines that can be applicable to all people, although, fortunately, there are a few remedial actions that can act very much like some of the new, broad-based "miracle drugs," in that they counteract a wide variety of problems. However, more of that later.

The uniqueness of the individual personality and the complexity of the world in which we live dictate that the specific events which occur in the person's life are bound to be different, one person to the next, and it is in that light that the situation must be viewed.

Recognizing that the symptoms will quite probably appear differently in different people, I have classified the various symptoms into two categories. The basis for classification rests on whether the symptom *primarily* functions within the individual or whether it is *primarily* displayed outwardly in terms of overt behavior. No one symptom fits purely into either class. To debate the classification of any one symptom would be an exercise in both futility and stupidity.

A. Personality-Oriented Symptoms

1. Unhappiness. Although perhaps one of the least specific of the symptoms of the Mid-Life Crisis, a generally unhappy life or a state of general unhappiness is the most common.

The dramatic and traumatic symptoms of divorce, infidelity, performance ineffectiveness, and alcoholism (to mention but a few) are generally visible, and to those of us who work in the field, commonplace. However, there is a far greater incidence of general unhappiness that does not culminate in climactic and disastrous events. Rather, the individual (as well as those around him) continues to grind through life, finding enjoyment in little if anything and generally feeling miserable. Most characteristically, people with this problem live lives of hopelessness and helplessness, looking forward to little more than additional years of the same thing.

Although I do not have statistics on the matter, an uncommonly large proportion of the people with whom I speak spend their lives between required work, watching television, and sleep. The unhappy person sees his job as a requirement to survival, and generally treats it as such. As might be expected, absenteeism is frequently a problem, performance effectiveness is minimal, and the waste of talent is extreme.

This symptom proves my point—that the word *crisis*, with its emphasis in meaning on an identifiable turning point, is inadequate to the task of describing the broad array of problems that emanate from the same base causes and that exert influences which can and frequently do affect the entire remainder of a person's life.

In my experience, everyone suffering from mid-life problems experiences some degree of unhappiness. For some, the unhappiness itself is *the* major symptom.

There is an old cliche that it is lonely at the top. The point of this statement is that the final and ultimate responsibility for the organization over which the individual exercises authority rests with the person in charge, be he a general, chief executive officer, or someone with similar powers. In an entirely different sense, there is a true unhappiness and loneliness in far too many senior executives, born out of the success they have achieved. In the process of becoming successful, their sense of values has shifted to the point that accomplishment of material goals (achievement) becomes primary, and everything else is subordinated to it. Accordingly, emotion becomes a sign of weakness and self-sufficiency a major virtue.

A result of this transformation is that the executive loses his ability to empathize with others, but not only can he not share the feelings of others, he loses touch with his own.

The final result, too frequently, is the successful executive who is strong, decisive, able to help and guide others—truly the master of his fate and captain of his soul. The obeisance paid him by others fosters and strengthens this attitude.

By-products of the executive's success frequently include real loneliness because he has no one he can talk to or share his feelings with, for to do either would be to suggest that he is human and thus imply a weakness.

Success and achievement do not need to be accompanied by a loss of the ability to feel. Nor are human compassion and the ability to make tough personnel decisions incompatible. I have maintained for many years that decisions affecting other people can and should be made in two steps. First, the necessary decision should be reached strictly on the basis of the facts present in the situation, without regard for any emotional involvement. The second step involves the decision as to how to carry out the first decision, and this should take into account human feelings and all other relevant related elements. Thus a decision may well be required to fire someone, and that conclusion should be reached without regard for any personal feelings that might be involved. Once the decision is made, however, the action taken should recognize fully that a human being is involved and that a lack of compassion may create problems far exceeding the trauma of the termination itself.

However, the unhappy executive will frequently make the first decision and act on it directly without regard for the second—the human aspect of the situation.

As I have spoken with executives over the past 25 to 30 years, it has been commonplace to find very sucessful men who are desperately seeking for something of value which they have begun to realize has been lost along the way on their path to success. Some of the places that are examined in this search range from the extremes of formal religion, neighborhood Bible study groups, psychiatry, and the counsel of a good friend, to alcohol, an extra-marital affair, or joining with an extremist group operating on the lunatic fringe.

Tragedy, frequently, proves to be a major benefit in this situation. Divorce, loss of a job, a heart attack, any one frequently brings on a realization of what has happened in the person's life and can bring about an examination or reexamination of one's values.

2. Insecurity. All people strive for security. Considering the fragility of human life, real security is almost impossible to attain, at least by the material standards that are most frequently used in our society. The Mid-Life Crisis complicates this situation. For purposes of discussion, three aspects of security can be considered separately. These are

a. *Financial Security*: Under normal circumstances, very few people are completely free of material insecurity. Beyond the "normal" concerns about one's material welfare, many middle-agers show an abnormal fear of loss of job, which causes them to work harder than they need to, worry excessively, and accept indignities that debase their self-image and yet are considered necessary to job retention. (It is somewhat shocking to the old guard in top management these days to come face to face with young and secure employees who are willing to say, "That's ridiculous!" and refuse to go along with such practices. If the boss decides he likes such independence and asks accusingly of his older subordinates, "Why aren't you like that?", he creates further insecurity by failing to recognize the conditions the middle agers grew up in and what he would have done had they so behaved.)

b. *The Security of Belonging:* Man is by nature a gregarious animal. He finds fulfillment in the company of his fellows and strength in the security of those relationships. Mid-life problems frequently lead to alienation and isolation. The middle-ager finds himself in conflict even with his closest friends as, with age, he becomes more sensitive to criticism, stronger in the depth of his own feelings, and less flexible in dealing with change. This can even extend to the family. For example, in the family of the average executive, the husband/father spends the bulk of his time in the business world, where standards are harsh and unforgiving. He wants to help his children to be prepared to live in that environment, which someday they must. In the same family, the wife/mother sees less of the world's standards and knows the children far more intimately than the father does. Conflict results when the father, at home, criticizes the children's behavior in an attempt to help them prepare for the world in which they must live as adults, and the mother defends them on the basis of her intimate knowledge of their intentions as well as their behavior, and her ignorance of the outside world. In her defense of the children, the wife aligns herself with them and against her husband. The result often is alienation and conflict in one form or another, with the ultimate result that he is driven from the family circle, with all of the consequences of that flight. The real problem here is that he is unable to cope with the situation because of lack of flexibility, sees alienation where it does not exist; nevertheless the end result is the same.

c. *Personal, Emotional Insecurity:* One characteristic of the middle-ager is that as he continues to grow older he begins to have self-doubts about himself in many areas. One consequence of this is that many middle-agers develop a strong fantasy life and will even identify with young men who "appear" to "have it all together"—the guy whom girls fall over in a day of sexual liberation. Too frequently, he tries to emulate the behavior of the ideal with whom he identifies, by having an affair, contracting venereal disease, or by suffering the ridicule of those whose attitudes can and do affect his life. On the other hand, because of his self-doubts, a man may become impotent or semi-impotent, especially if his wife is not sensitive to his needs and does nothing to help him. (Sensitivity to each other's sexual needs is, of course, a major factor in any happy marriage.) Poorly responded to, especially at mid-life, such unfulfilled needs can create major problems. All too often, because of his ego, the male middle-ager cannot ask for what he needs. Thus he and his wife simply drift apart. The impact on his self-confidence can then expand, extending into other areas as well as remain localized, where it is apt to find expression in cynicism or some other type of familial-destructive behavior.

3. Depression. Depression has become such a problem in our society today that it is almost epidemic. As they enter their 30s and 40s, many people experience conflict between what they *have* to do, on their jobs, and what they would like to do. Depression follows, along with other self-destructive behaviors when the size of the gap becomes apparent *and* it appears that the gulf can never be bridged.

As mentioned previously, some middle-aged executives

wake up one day to find that in achieving success they have paid the price of growing apart from their families, and conclude (rightly or wrongly) that nothing can be done.

Further, many middle-agers have achieved their initial career goals, have recognized that setting higher goals may not be realistic, and, feeling "trapped" by their responsibilities, can see no other avenue to pursue. Faced, then, with a belief that life has become a treadmill, depression ensues.

For our purposes here, suffice it to say that depression can be defined as extreme unhappiness, inactivity (or ineffective behavior), and gloominess in outlook.

The extensiveness of this problem on the American scene is exemplified by the fact that during one short period while this book was being written, three television specials, several radio shows, and a number of Sunday supplement and special articles in the newspaper all "happened" to appear.

4. Indecision. As an outgrowth of insecurity on the one hand and depression on the other, many middle-agers exhibit indecisiveness. Whether it be because of a fear of the consequences of taking a stand or whether it is the result of a lassitude growing out of a depressed state, the end effect is the same.

5. Fear and Anxiety. As is seen later when mid-life problem causes are being discussed, fears of various sorts are at the root of more crises than is almost anything else. At the same time, fear and anxiety themselves are symptoms of mid-life problems and are reported widely by those experiencing difficulty.

Anxiety is normally defined as a sense of impending disaster, and that is exactly what the person feels. Without knowing why, he feels that something bad is going to happen and, (like depression) that feeling exerts a pall over all that he does.

6. Conflict. There are a number of conflicts that are age related. Perhaps the most prominent of these is the conflict that the middle-ager feels between what he knows he is and what he would like to be. This is important only because at the same time he begins to recognize that his opportunities to become what he would like to be are diminishing rapidly and, in most cases, are assumed to have disappeared altogether. The phrase, "Well, I guess I'm over-the-hill," is not just an idle jest. Many people who say it are expressing the resolution of the conflict and a resignation (erroneous) to what they feel has to be.

There is another type of conflict that creates problems for the middle-ager and often leads to a crisis. A good way to exemplify it is to draw a parallel between the transition that is a part of adolescence and that which is also a part of middle age. For example, adolescence is a time of transition from childhood to adulthood, a time that is characterized by a trial-and-error approach to assumed responsibility and the testing of authority. There is a great deal of "approach-avoidance" behavior, in which the child is attracted by the glamour of "being a grownup," but is repelled by the responsibilities of adulthood. Having the "right" to make your own decisions is great, but the obligation of living with the results of those decisions is too painful to be acceptable in far too many cases. Thus there is conflict.

During adolescence there is *also* a great deal of "approach-approach" behavior. The pleasures of the irresponsibility of childhood are equally attractive to the *assumed* joys of the "freedom" of adulthood. The adolescent is torn in both directions simultaneously, and again conflict results, this time from a choice between two equally attractive alternatives.

Middle age is also a transition. It is a transition, however, of a different sort and magnitude, since there is very little of the "approach-approach" aspect of the situation (no one wants to grow old). There is a great deal of the "approach-avoidance" type of behavior, however, for people do want to continue growing, but they don't want to do so at the expense or cost of continuing the aging process. With deliberate redundancy, the concept of middle age as a transition is important from another standpoint. The Mid-Life Crisis is, for most people, a transitory thing that does not last for a particularly long time.

The problem with the crisis, though, rests in the consequences of the behavior that results from the pressures during the time the crisis is at its peak. For example, the enduring consequences of alcoholism, impulsive job changes, unhappy marriages, divorce, and destroyed interpersonal relationships do not cease with the passing of the crisis itself and can continue through the rest of a person's life.

7. Nervousness. Many people who experience mid-life problems report that, "My nerves seem to be on edge." The volume of smoking increases, alcoholic intake goes up, general tension rises. The consequence of these behaviors on interpersonal relationships is obvious, and the effects likewise so.

8. Restlessness. In one sense, this reported symptom differs very little from the symptom of nervousness. On the other hand, it is noted separately only to suggest that some people with whom I have spoken describe their symptoms as more an inability to concentrate on any one thing or retain interest in anything for very long as opposed to a nervousness, which has more of a depression-related aspect to it. The restless person may drive his close associates nuts, but more importantly, he will find it difficult to focus attention on long, involved tasks and will feel an excessive need for physical activity. To the extent that the latter can be focused into constructive channels, it can be good. However, more often than not, it ends in jumping from one thing to another, with little constructive accomplishment.

9. A Feeling of Being Trapped. Perhaps one of the most commonly reported symptoms of mid-life is that of being so "hemmed in" by one's responsibilities and obligations that the person's individuality disappears.

Although few are able to say it this succinctly, a typical statement would be, "I have so much time invested in my job now that I can't leave, and even if I could, I'm too old to learn a new profession, and if I tried, how would I support my family, pay the mortgage, and put something away for the kids' college education and our retirement?". It is perfectly normal to want to do other things and to wonder whether one could be successful in another career, but here the problem is of a different sort. Once the individual realizes that he has reached a point of no return, the feeling of entrapment can make what is otherwise a very satisfying job and personal situation seem as though it were not. Accordingly, from the feeling of being trapped, the job becomes less satisfying, and some feelings of resentment toward family are built.

10. Obsession with Death, Illness, and Old Age. When some people recognize the inevitability of death, the irresistible advance of age, and the increasing likelihood of serious illness, those very thoughts dominate their thinking. In a sense, it is a sort of depression (certainly the end result is the same), and far too great a portion of their time is devoted to negative things at the expense of all that is positive.

B. Behavioral Symptoms

1. Irrational Job Changes. This "symptom" of the Mid-Life Crisis is an excellent example of the complex intermingling of symptoms and causes in this area. One visible behavior symptom is the fact of the job change itself, and the key is that the reasons for it are irrational (and I recognize that the word is rather strong). It is extremely important to not get caught up in a semantic problem at this point, nor to be overly perfectionistic and pure about labeling or classifying "symptoms" and "causes." It is much more important to look at the behaviors involved, attempt to understand them, and from this learn how to overcome the problem. The job change is usually brought about by fear, and the fear is itself both a symptom and a cause. (Of course, some job changes should be made. My objection is to those that result from an emotional reaction rather than a calm reasoned decision.) Rash job changes take two basic forms. First, the individual will move to another job, usually without justification for leaving the one he has. The new job may be an identical position in the same field with the same sort of organization, or it may be in an entirely new field and even an entirely different job. Although it happens, it is unusual for the president of a company to resign that position and become a laborer. It is becoming less uncommon for someone to leave a job in which he has seniority and security such as that of a vice presidency to buy a boat livery or a gas station. Irrational job changes are seldom that dramatic, but they do occur frequently and in many ways.

The second type of rash job change is usually not thought of as such. In this case, the individual has reached a point, usually in middle management, where, on the basis of ability and/or inclination, he should remain. Nevertheless, driven by the fear of being fired if he doesn't continue to advance or by a need to prove that he is still growing and not "over-the-hill," he will push on to a higher level job. In the new position, the executive is frequently very unhappy and shares that unhappiness (whether they want it or not) with his family, friends, co-workers, and subordinates.

In my experience, a great many executives are quite unhappy in their positions, either because they recognize that they are not qualified for their jobs (it does not follow that all are necessarily able to admit this to themselves) or because the demands of the position are contrary to their personal interests. Nevertheless, driven by the factors cited above, they move on to jobs for which they are ill-suited, and in such a situation everybody (including the employer) loses.

This matter of middle-management promotions and promotability is very complex. (As is true with many other points in this book, to explore each item thoroughly would result in a multi-volumed book, and, more importantly, the main thought of the Mid-Life Crisis would be obscured.) Entangled with the Mid-Life Crisis problems of the middle manager are other problems: obsolescence, the fact that some middle managers are not promotable under any circumstances, the case of the middle manager being already one step ahead of where he should be, and the limited number of positions available at the top.

An example of this latter point is a middle-ager who, until fairly recently, was the manager of a department in a medium-size manufacturing concern. As such, he was quite effective, since he was able to run his relatively small department effectively through the use of good interpersonal relationships and a shirt-sleeve approach to the job. There is every reason to believe that had the situation remained as it was, he could have worked through to retirement as a productive member of middle management and earned enough to satisfy all of his and his family's needs. However, he saw his remaining in that position as an admission of his career having reached an end and found that to be both frightening and unacceptable. As a consequence, he began, openly, working for a vice presidency and, even though top management was not convinced of his capabilities for such responsibility, they rewarded his efforts with the promotion.

Now, he is over his head and is experiencing considerable difficulty, and top management is having second thoughts. Since his company does not believe in demotions, it is entirely probable that he will be asked to resign. It is also very probable that a very limited amount of career counseling could have avoided the problem in the first place.

2. Reduction in Productivity. Performance effectiveness and losses in productivity are very difficult to measure for a great many people. The problem is not inherent in the type of work a person does, but the fact that very few organizations employ effective performance appraisal methods, if any at all.

The fact remains, however, that when a person's attention is distracted from what he is doing and/or if he is worried about something, he will not do his work as well or in the quantity that would be true otherwise.

I do not know of any way to measure the productivity loss our nation suffers each year because of mid-life problems, but considering the widespread nature of them, the cost must be enormous.

This fact—productivity—is a major concern of this entire book. A great deal of space is not required, however, to set forth the essential facts and to identify the problem that is of major concern.

a. Few organizations have realistic, meaningful measures of executive productivity.

b. We have known for many years that off-the-job problems have a detectable effect on on-the-job performance. Even without the existing research results, sheer common sense would be sufficient proof to know that a person cannot concentrate on one thing when something he considers to be of greater importance is bothering him.

c. The cost to the organization must be measured both in terms of mistakes that are made (acts of commission) and things that are not done (acts of omission).

• The executive who is worried about the quality of his work will quite probably waste time checking and rechecking what he does and will avoid taking a risk that could ultimately benefit the company.

• The manager who is worried about his health will probably not be available to his subordinates as often as he should be, and thus actions will be taken without his knowledge or guidance.

• The depressed executive will not stand up and argue for even those things about which he feels strongly, and the best interests of his organization will thus not be defended.

• The man who holds resentment for the organization or his superiors will probably "hold back" from taking an action that will make them look good. If the attitude is held toward peers or subordinates, he will undoubtedly let (or even help) them to make mistakes. (I am reminded of the recently fired junior executive who gave vent to his resentment by performing highly accurate but irrelevant analyses of important data. He claimed that he was following orders. Since the orders had been given orally, his boss could not prove otherwise. Irretrievable time was lost, deadlines were missed and everyone came off a loser.)

Once again, I could cite many other examples, but I believe the point has been made. An executive's performance, in large part, is dependent on how he feels and his state of mind. As these are affected negatively by such things as the Mid-Life Crisis, his work suffers, productivity drops, and all concerned pay the price.

3. Resentment. It is literally impossible to distinguish between resentment as a symptom or a cause of mid-life problems. In a very real sense, it is the result (symptom) of other actions, but then itself serves to cause still other behavior. For that reason, it is dealt with, at length, in the section under emotional causes of mid-life problems. Suffice it to say here, that many middle-agers express resentment toward their families, employers, jobs, superiors, subordinates, co-workers, and even the world in general. This resentment is not always without justification, except perhaps in terms of its degree of expression and the fact that little or no constructive action is directed toward resolving it.

4. Retreat from Responsibility. Responsibility requires decision making, the exercise of authority, and some type of positive action. Under the pressures of mid-life problems, many people retreat from responsibility and actively seek ways of avoiding that for which they are accountable.

For example, a good executive must take risks. Insecurity will lead an executive to be cautious in his decision making, and it is almost an axiom that the "safe way" is not always the best way. Moreover, in a crisis some executives who are fearful of their jobs "freeze." They literally hide in their offices and avoid doing the very thing that would provide the security they so desire.

Given two alternatives, the executive who is afraid for his job will concentrate on the lesser of the two (the task more likely to be successful), even though the rewards would be greater if he were to choose the other alternative.

In today's business community there are many ways in which an executive can retreat from responsibility. For example, one very acceptable method is to delegate your responsibility to your subordinates. Since delegation is something that too many managers do inadequately, it is entirely possible that the middle-ager can get away with this for a long time without detection. Many readers are at this point, I am sure, questioning the use of delegation as a means of a retreat from responsibility. The point is that proper delegation has well-defined limits. The middle-ager who is in trouble will delegate in a manner that is better described as abdication and, when something goes wrong, is usually quick to place all of the blame on the subordinate.

It is somewhat ironical that bad management can so easily pass for good management (and so often does) until a crisis occurs that reveals what has been going on.

5. Alcohol. The use of alcohol as a beverage is so widespread and individual tolerances are so variable that it can be used to excess by some people for a long time without detection. Eventually, however, it usually comes to light and in one way or another effects both job performance and the alcoholic's private life.

Alcoholism is such a major problem that there is no need to spend time here describing what is common knowledge, beyond stating that as a symptom of mid-life problems it is commonplace.

6. Infidelity. The man who feels that his wife is unresponsive or fears that his virility is fading or wants "one more fling" before becoming a has-been or drinks too much because of job pressures, among a great many other reasons, may be unfaithful to his wife. This symptom is discussed in greater detail in the section devoted to emotional causes of mid-life problems.

7. Inconsistency of Behavior. Two truisms are often cited concerning human behavior. The first is that man's behavior is most consistent in its inconsistency. The second is that there is a basic consistency to each individual's overall pattern of behavior. Recognizing that both statements are true, middle-agers in trouble frequently exhibit behaviors that are quite inconsistent from those that their associates have come to expect of them.

For example, the person who has always worked long hours may begin following a straight 9:00 to 5:00 routine or the opposite. The manager who was always understanding about mistakes and errors could become a perfectionist and demand nothing less. The conservative could become a liberal and the radical a moderate. In each case, the change is sufficiently distinct to be noteworthy.

Under the pressures of our "youth culture" today, many middle-agers attempt to deny the aging process by letting their hair grow long, adopting jeans as a customary mode of dress, learn each new dance as it comes along, and support causes that even a moderate amount of rational thinking would reveal as untenable. Sometimes this behavior serves as a passing phase. In other instances it has led to back problems, alienation of friends and relatives, job loss, infidelity, alcoholism, and drug addiction.

8. Divorce. The nature of this symptom is so well known as to not require discussion.

We have reached a point in our society where, statistics show, just about as many divorces occur as do marriages. More important for our purposes here, is a growing epidemic of divorce in the middle years, along with an increasing evidence of each of the symptoms listed above. Every one of the foregoing symptoms, both personality oriented and behavioral, lacks uniqueness. Each can be found in a wide variety of situations as a result of a wide range of causes. The important point here is that each is the direct result of a middle-ager's concern with middle age and the consequences of having reached that point in life where what is ahead is at best no more than what lies behind and very likely will be less. To describe how problems can develop, I have put together a little five-act play that is based upon an uncomfortably large number of cases. It shows both the symptoms described above and serves as a prelude to the causes that will be described next, all of which relate to what has been termed the Mid-Life Crisis.

MID-LIFE CRISIS—FIVE-ACT PLAY

Setting: Anytown, U.S.A.
Characters: The average American couple

ACT I

He: Has a beginning level job and is working for advancement.
She: Fully occupied with the house and children. During these very early years, she may even be contributing financially through a job.
Keynote: Both are working together. They feel a strong sense of belongingness, since each is contributing to the growth, development, and welfare of their family.

ACT II

Keynote: The mid years

He: Still working—has achieved some measure of success, but finds now that he must run faster just to stay in place. It is not as easy for him to learn new technological advances as it once was (a combination of age and the development of other interests that interfere with his learning time). He is under great pressure from younger men who are sharp technologically and vigorous physically. He is beginning to see limited opportunities for further advancement and some threat to even maintaining the position he has already achieved. Work is beginning to become work—not always fun or satisfying in and of itself as it has been in the past. (In our society, men's lives are generally *job* oriented. Most men report a strong correlation between age and job pressures.)

She: The children no longer take so much of her time, so to occupy herself she turns to other diversions both inside and outside the home. She has plenty of time for television and entertaining, and outside the home can join clubs, do volunteer work, return to work and so on. (Women's lives in our society are generally *family* oriented. They report "freedom" from the restrictions of those responsibilities as the hallmark of the middle years.)

ACT III

Keynote: Later in the middle years.

He: More frequently he comes home tired, worried, and insecure. (At this point, it might be worthwhile to add the factor of male menopause, with its emotional and physiological consequences, when this factor is better understood.)

She: With her freedom fairly well solidified, she has probably found a number of things she enjoys doing. If he has been financially successful, she, very likely, is enjoying the fruits of his success (perhaps she is spending a great deal of time at their country club) and is involved in all of the many things that he would like to do but for which he cannot find time. (The factor of female menopause with its physiological and emotional consequences must also be taken into account here.)

ACT IV

Keynote: August 15th, 7:00 P.M. He has just arrived home.

He: Resents the fact that they are no longer working together. He is doing it all with no emotional support from her, while she is having a ball.

She: Sees her own problems of middle age, she feels that she deserves an opportunity to enjoy herself, because during the early years when he was "only working," she was also working all day long, generally spending longer hours than he with housework and also taking care of the children at night. Moreover, she resents his resentment.

He: May be slowing down sexually, but because of male ego wants to prove that he is still as capable as he once was.

He: Instead of receiving the comfort he so needs, he is faced with further evidence of how far their lives have grown apart. When they first were married, they had everything in common, and now have nothing.

They: The evening does not go too well. He resents what she is saying and talking about and feels far outside of the part of her life she finds most enjoyable. She finds him unresponsive, quiet, perhaps even sullen. By the time bedtime arrives, they are barely speaking to one another. If there is any sexual activity that night, it is probably unsatisfactory for both, or possibly she rejects his advances with some excuse, and the foundation is laid for a wall that will grow up between them.

FOOTNOTE: The same process and the same result could occur if he were to arrive home with the needs mentioned above and be met with a demand that he take some disciplinary action for the children or engage in some other activity which he finds onerous or disagreeable.

She: Quite probably less interested in sex than he is—since she feels no need to "prove herself," she is probably not as responsive as she once was.

He: Feels rejected emotionally and physically.

She: Despite her greater freedom and opportunity for enjoyment, has strong needs for emotional support.

He: He wants her to enjoy herself, but is jealous of her opportunity to do so while he can't. He feels guilty about his own resentment, and these guilt feelings are all mixed up with the many other pressures he faces.

At that point he comes home at night after having had a particularly bad day. He is out of sorts and feels a strong need for sympathy, understanding, and emotional support.

She: Meets him at the door with a bubbling, effervescent description of a very happy day. She feels so good that she wants to share her enjoyment with him and expects that he too will feel the same.

ACT V

Keynote: The next day at the office he asks his secretary (or female colleague) to work late to complete a project that is due. After finishing, he invites her out to dinner since, after all "they both have to eat," and it is "justifiable" because it is in partial payment for her having worked late.

He: At dinner he recognizes that his companion is someone with whom he has a great deal in common—much more than he has with his wife.

FOOTNOTE: This play, in the real world, has ended many ways. Some of the more common include:

1. A thoroughly unhappy couple living out an embittered existence.
2. Infidelity on the part of one, the other or both.
3. Divorce.
4. Desertion.
5. Alcoholism.

The ending in the individual case will be a result of the circumstances of the specific couple, their respective levels of emotional maturity, social pressures that are brought to bear on them, and so on.

A FINAL NOTE

It was clearly established, many years ago, that people are "whole beings." What happens to a person on the job affects his life off the job and vice versa. Thus job or career fears affect the individual's home and social lives. Conversely, problems in even the most intimate facet of a man's private life will be reflected on the job in some way and to some extent.

Depression is generalized over everything a person does. Family troubles go with a man into his office. Indeed, alcoholism, infidelity, boredom, frustration, fears, insecurity, impotence (real or imagined), marital disharmony—to mention but a few effects—reduce employee productivity by hundreds of thousands of hours every year.

The impact on all employees is great. However, the greatest effect is found with those who have a measure of control over their performance and the cost there is incalculable.

For example, the employee on the production line who has a family problem may damage some equipment, products, or even himself. The costs involved will be relatively minor. If he becomes an alcoholic or has an affair—without in any way attempting to demean the cost in human terms for those involved—once again the impact will not be particularly noticeable *to the organization*. With an executive, however, a million dollar contract missed, a personal problem that reflects on the image of the entire organization, or an entire unit that (because of poor leadership) operates at only half of its normal effectiveness, the costs can be staggering.

For these reasons, it is shocking that so few organizations are concerned even to the point of taking the very inexpensive steps that are necessary to prevent the problems in the first place or deal with them head on once they have occurred.

Indeed, in particularly bad situations, a typical organization reaction is to fire the employee involved (blue collar or executive). This has the advantage of eliminating the problem and immediately reducing the cost. However, one major contributing cause to the Mid-Life Crisis for many employees is poor management, and "firing the victim" is not a very satisfactory solution to the problem.

Having dealt directly with top management for more than 25 years in every type of industry and with organizations ranging from the mega giants to the small, family-owned businesses, I am intimately familiar with the attitude of management toward problems of the sort listed here. It will take an enlightened executive—a very rare breed indeed—to recognize that:

- The normal view of the organization from a top management position is murky at best.
- The greatest skill of some of the most effective executives is that of hiding their incompetence.
- The major cost of poor management is found in unrealized profits.

• Despite the jokes made about it, communication in any organization will be poor unless extensive, continuous attention is paid to it; whatever it costs to maintain effective communications will be more than paid for out of increased profits (or reduced costs, however the accounting is done).

ANOTHER REDUNDANCY

On the other hand—in contrast to all of the foregoing—for reasons that will be noted later, there are people who find opportunity rather than danger in the mid-life period. These people see it as a time for constructive reappraisal, rededication and renewed enthusiasm; with resulting increased productivity, improved job satisfaction, personal growth and real achievement.

4 Causes of Mid-Life Problems

(Symptoms?)

It is impossible to find very many individual human behaviors that are the result of only one cause. Precipitating factors may be unitary, but contributing causes are generally many.

For example, in the news in recent years increasing space has been given to descriptions of the vast number of child beatings and wife beatings that occur daily. The uninformed frequently cry out for social scientists to identify "the" cause of this behavior, when in fact, the causes are many and the precipitating incidents are infinite. I do not pretend to have "the" answer here, but common sense alone should reveal part of the problem. That is to say, because of individual problems, it would take a multi-volumed book to cite the many causes that are involved, but it is very easy to recognize that the social changes of the past few years have created a problem for many men. Among these can be included the constant frustration each person faces daily in almost everything he does, the very visible moral decline in our society, the steadily mounting injustices that are so much a part of modern life, the lenient treatment of offenders by the courts, the male's intellectual unpreparedness for women's liberation, the lack of concern for the personhood of so many by so many, and so on and so on. For many years we have known that frustration leads to aggression and that aggression is most often focused on "safe" objects that cannot be aggressive in return. The result is easy to predict.

In exactly the same manner, the fact of individual differences in mid-life problems, their intensity, nature, and number are well established, although patterns of onset are highly individualized. In general, though, there is a growth of one (or more) major cause that sets the stage (cocks the gun). That cause or those causes can build until an explosion erupts. On the other hand, in more and more cases it appears that the major causes are aggravated by the "big pressure" of cumulative, tiny events—for example, the minor, never-ending daily rip-offs that beset everyone, as mentioned previously. When the explosion occurs, the precipitating incident may be something so minor and trivial that it seems to defy reason, and, viewed alone, it does. Seen as the final bit of pressure, however, it is the trigger that trips the hammer, and the gun goes off.

To look at the problem from still another viewpoint, the causes of mid-life problems are interactive and highly related to individual differences. Thus, your situation is unique. Because of that fact:

a. It is meaningless for you to look for the thing that seems to affect the "average person," since you are you and not the average person.

b. It is equally meaningless to attempt to relate events in your life to some specific age or age range. The problem with that approach is that by looking for some specific thing, your self-examination will thus be biased by your expectation for the thing you are seeking. More importantly, on not finding it, you might delude yourself into thinking that you are "home free" when, in fact, quite the opposite may be true. Ever since I became identified with the Mid-Life Crisis concept, I have been beset by two references to age.

• The standard first question from everyone is, "What is the age at which it will hit?" As you can note through repeated references throughout this book, this question is meaningless. To satisfy the many questionners, though, I finally began giving the age range of 35 to 55 and added to this, many many caveats.

• As might be expected, the caveats are seldom heard, and the statements I now hear are either, "Well, I haven't hit my crisis yet," or "Since I'm past 55, I guess I'm safe." Both statements, in terms of the real facts, are ridiculous. And it is for this reason that I believe it is so essential to think in terms of mid-life problems (problems that are related to your conception of age and your life) and not in terms of a specific crisis or point in time.

c. Look at yourself! You are unique! You are "one of a kind!" What affects other people one way very probably will affect you differently. No one but you has ever lived your life and had your experiences.

THE CAUSES

Once again, we have a classification problem. For purposes of discussion, I have divided the basic causes of mid-life problems (and the Mid-Life Crisis) into three categories:

- Physical causes
- Environmental causes
- Emotional causes

As these are discussed there will be some crossing over between categories. However, it is much more important to keep in mind that the individual causes interact with one another, and all of these singly and in concert are set within the unique set of characteristics that is the individual.

A. Physical Causes

The physical *symptoms* of advancing age are causes of middle-age problems and of the Mid-Life Crisis.

1. The Specific Physiological Changes with Age

- Loss of hair
- Reduction of physical strength
- An increased need for rest and sleep
- In some cases a decreased need for sleep or a change in the amount of sleep required at any one time
- A reduction in the strength of the sex drive
- A tendency toward gaining weight
- A loss of visual acuity
- An increase in the number and severity of physical ailments
- A loss of hearing
- A change of hair color to gray

2. Knowledge of the Aging Process. Over the years, some attention has been given to the aging process in women, particularly as it is related to menopause. Even there, however, it is obvious that there is a vast area of needed research and a great deal of knowledge that has yet to be acquired.

As far as men are concerned, aside from the fact that men indeed do grow older, very little is known of the aging process in general.

I am not a physician and will not become involved in a medical argument. From the many men I have talked to, however, it is clear that there is a process that goes on during middle age (possibly hormonal in nature and comparable to female menopause) that results in the visible evidence of aging and which very likely has an emotional counterpart as well. In one sense, it would appear that "male menopause," if there is such a thing, is almost the other side of puberty.

Studying the problem in men is difficult. The reasons for this are

a. Individual differences in the aging process are dramatic. Some people become bald at age 30; others die at a very advanced age with a full head of hair. Differences in hair color at various ages are substantial; physical fitness (vis-a-vis the middle-age paunch) are strikingly varied; the strength of the sex drive (so closely related to emotional factors) differs widely from one man to another; and so on.

b. Many men hide the more important and significant consequences of "male menopause" and thus any attempt to study it is hampered. It is not significant to our purpose here to explore this point in great detail. However, suffice it to say that the physiological changes with age should be fairly easy to examine. On the other hand, the physical and the emotional factors are so closely tied together that one cannot be researched without considering both. The difficulties arise when certain sensitive areas are approached. For example, it is not "manly" in our society to cry, and rapid swings of temperament are not nearly as acceptable in men as they are in women. Also, some of the research will probably have to wait until someone can find a profit in it, but when it is done, it should be of great value.

3. Why are Physiological Changes Important? The physical and physiological changes that occur in middle age are not, in and of themselves, important as causes of either the Mid-Life Crisis or of mid-life problems. What is important is the reaction to these changes that occurs, since they signify a number of things many people consider to be of extreme importance. Among the more obvious of these are the following:

a. The physiological changes that occur in middle age are signs (that cannot be ignored) of advancing old age. Most people in our society consider old age to be a tragedy and thus something to be avoided or denied at almost any cost. Common reactions to these signs are found in innumerable cases such as:

• One man considered a *perceived* reduction in his sex drive as a loss of his "manhood" and from this developed a substantial inferiority complex.
• There is a large industry devoted to returning hair color from gray back to its former shade.
• The head of a small agency felt that his sex drive was diminishing and attempted to prove this to be false by increasing his sexual activity with his wife. The result was

an unwanted middle-age pregnancy and a very unhappy change in a number of long-term plans.

• A woman in her middle years found that a drink or two before bedtime was an aid to sleep and from that beginning has gone on to become a full-blown alcoholic.

• Millions upon millions of dollars are spent annually for phony remedies to counteract problems related to menopause, overweight, loss of vitality, and ailments real and imagined.

b. The physical changes of middle age are an undeniable sign of eventual death. Most people consider death to be such a horrible calamity that even thinking about it is to be avoided at all costs. (This is dealt with later on in greater detail.)

4. Summary. No matter how hard one may try, the aging process cannot be stopped. Viewed in the negative manner of the cases listed above, it is a major problem. On the other hand, a change of attitude will usually eliminate most of the problems that result from physical causes of mid-life problems, and, as difficult as it might be to believe at this juncture, those changes can produce positive rather than negative results, if properly approached.

B. Environmental Causes

It is almost impossible to treat this category of causes apart from the one that follows—emotional causes. Indeed, in the final analysis, the major distinction between the environmental and the emotional is that most of the environmental changes begin outside of the person, whereas those I have classified as "emotional" are inwardly generated.

Keeping this distinction in mind, there are three broad categories of environmental causes from which almost no one is immune. These are

1. Job Pressures. The middle-ager does not react as well to pressure as he did when he was younger. Unfortunately, the more successful he becomes and the higher he goes in the organizational hierarchy, the more the pressure increases.

Proof of the existence of that pressure once again can be seen in the number of articles, books, and television programs (to mention only three) that are devoted to the end product of pressure: stress. Once more, the severity of the problem is reflected in the reactions to it. One consequence of stress is overeating, and obesity is considered to be a national problem. A second reaction to stress is high blood pressure (at least in part), and today high blood pressure is such a problem that you can have your blood pressure taken on a street corner in a mobile "blood pressure trailer" in many places. Third, alcohol is the answer that far too many executives find for stress, and the number of alcoholics in this country is shocking.

Stress and its effects build silently. Many people have told me that when they first found that they had been affected by stress, they did so with considerable surprise. Most frequently, the signs are visible to others before they are to the victim. By the time things are bad enough that you notice the problem yourself, considerable effort will be required to overcome the problem.

A few of the sources of pressure on the job, for the middle ager are

a. *Growing Responsibility:* Almost without exception, jobs today are becoming more and more complex, in and of themselves, without expansion, through increasing the number of duties. This is particularly true of executive positions. For example, government regulations require that an ever-increasing number of forms be completed, recordkeeping be expanded, and laws be understood and obeyed. The entire manner in which business is conducted has changed radically in the last few years, and there is good cause to believe that it will continue to change as radically as time goes on.

b. All the costs involved in doing business have skyrocketed, and to make a profit is a growing challenge.

c. A great deal of social legislation, although necessary and highly desirable, creates innumerable problems of implementation on the job.

d. The attitudes of many younger employees are quite at variance with those of the middle-aged manager, and this adds to his burden.

e. The knowledge explosion continues, and the rate of change in technology within every profession is increasing. When the executive is reaching the peak of his career and would like to spend a little more time relaxing and enjoying his success, the pressures mount for him to retain what he has achieved and even to go forward. (We have an odd psychology in this country that a person must constantly strive to continue to advance—perhaps in fear that if he does not, he will begin to slide backward. Under the proper conditions, most people could be productive and yet content to remain in a static position without advancement from some point to the end of their careers.)

Young people are graduated from college today with as much usable information as many executives have, even though it took the executives 20 years to acquire that knowledge. Obsolescence thus becomes another job pressure, one that merits special mention because of the way it is treated. Many organizations require that top executives remain technically "current," even though their jobs would be best served if they used their time to "manage" technically competent subordinates. One has to wonder what advantage accrues to an organization that sends a 64-year-old senior vice president to a technical training program. What really *is* the basic philosophy of an organization that requires top management to retain technological skills that are seldom if ever used or that permits those same people to apply management methods that went out of date with the spinning wheel?

f. With all that I have said previously, there is another phenomenon which is beginning to become evident with respect to employees who are within a few years of retirement—surprisingly, often as many as 10 years out. This phenomenon can be best described as one in which the employee is ignored when promotions are available, is taken for granted, or is thought of as "too old" to be productive in a truly challenging situation. Unfortunately, the end result of this situation is usually not a happy one *for the organization*. The talent, skill, energy, and ability that *could* be the employer's are vented off in civic activities, social affairs, religious organizations, or personal hobbies that are of little benefit to the organization or perhaps even to the individual. The job, in many cases, becomes a "necessary evil" to provide support for the employee—a place in which he will "work out" his retirement and then leave with relief. In the meantime, the organization and its stockholders have suffered a substantial loss.

2. Changes in Society. Most of today's middle-agers grew up in a world that had a discernibly defined structure centered on a value system that had general community acceptance. Amid the horrendous problems, hard times, and all the bad things we like to forget with the passing years, there was at the same time a fairly well-defined line between right and wrong. You and your neighbors shared an agreement as to what fell on either side. Those who committed wrongs were not only looked on as lawbreakers but were also subject to social ostracism—authority was accorded a discernible respect—the family unit was relatively stable and secure—people, generally, would respond to a call for "help"—and the traditions and myths that so erroneously pass for the teachings of Moses and Christ exerted a positive, controlling influence on society, even though too often factually in error.

Today, all that has changed. Value systems differ not only from neighborhood to neighborhood, but from house to house. Even worse, the differences exist within families between generations. The middle-ager finds that his values—apparently—are shared by very few; his inability to articulate a religious faith prohibits him from talking about values with his friends and relatives; fear of ostracism and job insecurity keep him from telling his co-workers or boss how he feels; because of television and many other similar distractions, he has lost the ability to communicate with his family. In general, to quote our friends from Texas, he finds himself between a rock and a hard place.

3. Expectations of Others. Every human being plays a variety of roles in the various facets of his life. Those people who, by middle age, have achieved some prominence, are usually sought after by many people for many things.

The executive, particularly, is besieged by civic organizations for his participation through monetary contributions, committee memberships, elected office, and so on. There are always more jobs to be done than people to do them, and every organization wants to get the best people available.

Professional organizations and clubs also seek out those who have achieved some mark of success, and many individuals are quite expert at "conning" other people into doing not very desirable tasks.

Even family and friends are frequently on the doorstep of the middle-ager who has shown himself to be capable in one or more fields.

There is nothing wrong with asking people for help, and certainly the human ego is flattered when others call for use of one's talents. The problem comes when the entire matter gets out of proportion, and because he cannot say no to a worthy cause, a family member or friend, or the pleadings of an articulate "organizer" for a church, professional organization, or club, the middle-ager finds himself so overburdened that he does not have time to do justice to any of his responsibilities, and his actual contribution to all suffers.

The expectations of others is also a problem on another level—the control that others have over your life. For our purposes we are concerned with only two of those levels of control. First is the control you voluntarily give to those whom you accept as being competent to control your life (a surgeon, a cook in a restaurant, a taxicab driver, or an airline pilot).

Second, there are a great many instances in which you involuntarily find control of your life in the hands of others, and this leads to frustration in far too many cases, especially if the other person's life style differs from yours and conflict results through some negative impact on your choice of action. For example, you are in a single lane of traffic, and the person in the car ahead of you decides to stop to talk to a friend on the sidewalk, with complete disregard for your "rights" to proceed. If you object, he will undoubtedly become annoyed. As another example, it is Saturday morning (your only free day of the week), and one member of the family won't get out of bed so that you can plan what you will do that day as a family. In effect, that person controls your life at that point, and this can be frustrating—unfortunately, frustration often leads to anger and aggression. You feel you are not being given the respect due your age and position—you feel guilty over those self-serving feelings—and your spiral of conflicting emotions spins on. As a final example, you are a nonsmoker, sitting in a restaurant enjoying a good meal. Suddenly, someone sits down at the next table, and you find yourself in a cloud of cigarette smoke that destroys the taste of your food, causes your eyes to water, creates a breathing problem, and is doubly annoying since it affects your dinner companion the same way. When you object to the distress being caused by the smoke, the resulting conversation ruins your evening.

As you can see, the environmental causes are all wrapped up with emotions. Separation of the two is impossible.

C. Emotional Causes

The primary causes of the Mid-Life Crisis and all mid-life problems are essentially emotional in nature.

Redundancy

It is important that you maintain a clear picture of my distinction between the Mid-Life Crisis and mid-life problems. The key to the differences between the two hinges on the word *crisis* and that aspect of its definition that suggests something has occurred suddenly or has reached a point of being out of control.

With some exceptions, mid-life problems build slowly over a long period of time. You are not aware of their importance or significance until something happens (it can be anything) and then, all of a sudden, it all falls into place. It is *as though* something had actually happened at one point in time (although it didn't) just because the realization came in one flash of insight.

My seemingly undue concern for what might be felt to be a minor point is based on a fact of human nature. Too frequently, people feel that understanding something will cause it to "go away," or that a solution of the "quick fix" variety will eliminate the problem, again because it "seems so clear." Mid-life problems can be solved in a vast majority of cases, but usually dedicated effort and consistent attention are required over a long period of time, probably for the rest of your life.

During the past few years I have given many speeches on the Mid-Life Crisis, and an article containing many of the concepts included in this book was published some time ago. From this exposure I have had contact with several thousand people from all walks and stations of life through face-to-face conversation and telephone and mail communication.

Although these people do not constitute a scientifically selected sample of the general population, the group is large enough to give me the ability to predict the questions that will be asked and the attitudes that will be expressed with an extremely high degree of accuracy. Based on this background, plus more than 25 years of professional experience dealing with top- and middle-management persons (almost all of whom fall broadly into the middle-age group), I can speak with confidence about the way most middle agers view mid-life problems and, specifically, the Mid-Life Crisis.

The point I want to make is that in addition to looking for a "quick fix" solution to mid-life problems, there is a widely held belief that having a Mid-Life Crisis is like having the measles. Once over with, you are immune from that point on. Nothing could be further from the truth. Here again is my concern for that aspect of the definition of the word "crisis" that denotes something which occurs in a short space of time such as is true with a physical disorder that appears rapidly and is quickly cured.

Mid-life problems are a part of life. They do not cease or go away. *"The"* Mid-Life Crisis is a fallacy. You may have one *or* you may have many. The determining factors are to be found in your make-up and personality.

Specific Emotional Causes

As was noted earlier, emotional causes originate primarily within the individual, mainly as conclusions or beliefs that grow out of observations, specific experiences, introspection, or some combination of the three. It is difficult to rank order each of the causes in terms of importance, for what is most significant for one individual may have relatively little meaning for someone else. Accordingly, the order below does not denote significance.

1. Personal Adjustment. One of the two major keynotes as to how a person will deal with mid-life problems is found in the quality and nature of his personal adjustment or, if you prefer, his level of maturity.

Since there is no such thing as total maturity, the more mature person is better equipped to take mid-life problems in stride, deal with them as they occur, and experience a minimum of disruption to the course of his life than is the less mature person.

A complete catalog of all of the immature reactions to mid-life problems would be almost endless. A few examples should suffice to illustrate the point.

a. *Problems of Personal Identity:* (Note: The problem listed here is normal for an early teenager; in a person in their late teens or early 20s, it is a sign of retarded maturation; in a middle-ager it is immaturity at the level of a problem.) The person who has to ask the question, "Who am I?" has paid very little attention to himself and the world around him. Most likely, he has been running so rapidly "on a track to nowhere" that he has not been able to see where he has been. Another way of saying this is, "If you don't know where you're going you can't get lost, but neither will you ever arrive."

On the other hand, it is also possible that such a person is "copping out" to avoid accepting adult responsibility, or it might be that he is just simply too lazy to look.

The answer to this question will never come by going away for awhile. In terms of this specific problem, you are more likely to get your head together by working at it where you are and where you are going to have to live and eat for the rest of your life. Most people who take a year off to "find themselves" usually don't.

Being an adult is not easy! It is hard work and requires self-discipline. Thus, many "grown-ups" have never made it.

b. *Insecurity:* One obvious symptom of insecurity is indecision. There are, however, many others. For example, some people go to rather extreme lengths to obtain approval for what they do—even to the point of asking for it—whereas others seek or even demand visible evidence of respect. These are immature reactions.

c. *Depression:* This concept, previously discussed as a symptom of the Mid-Life Crisis, can also denote a lack of good personal adjustment, depending upon its intensity, duration, and scope. It is not immature to feel disheartened at failure; it is not immature to be even deeply saddened by a personal loss; and it is not immature to just simply "get the blues" for no apparent reason. When depression extends past a short time, however and becomes debilitating or limiting to the use of one's abilities (such as leading to a state of apathy), it is immature—or worse.

A form of immaturity that leads to depression (usually among those who see retirement coming even as far out as 10 years) involves a cross section of some of the causes listed in this chapter. In general, what is involved here is a growing dissatisfaction with one's work that is intermingled with obsolescence and any number of other factors such as:

- The job end is in sight and there are many unreached, unrealized goals on the job and in your career.
- The end of life is at least a conscious reality, with many unreached and unrealized life goals and dreams.
- While slowing down, you are being pushed by younger people. (As a waitress said to me the other day, "I have no trouble springing out of bed at 4:30 A.M. in the morning, but my bones do.")
- Ridiculous retirement policies and practices.

Everything seems to turn sour all at once.

d. *Escapism:* The definition of maturity is not clearly fixed and fully agreed to by all professional practitioners in the field of human behavior. One of the reasons for this is that most behaviors are perfectly normal within certain limits and become abnormal only beyond a particular point. The issue and controversy center on the fixing of that point. For example, it is normal for a person to want to escape from a situation that is unpleasant, one in which he faces constant frustration, a seemingly endless number of problems that must be solved, or even responsibility that will never permit him to relax. It is normal to want to be able to express your own individuality and to find refuge from people who are seemingly always "clawing at you for something." It is even mature (indeed, it is *very* mature) to arrange a means of relieving these pressures, but the point of immaturity is reached when the person abdicates his responsibilities, walks away from his problems without arranging for their solution, and completely disregards the consequences of his behavior.

e. *Jealousy and Suspicion:* A major, usually unrecognized cause of problems in long-term marriages—especially in those of successful executives—is the immature reaction of jealousy and/or suspicion.

The couple (very much like the five-act play cited earlier) began married life working together, but with time and success, things have changed. Her responsibilities have lessened.

She can spend more and more time enjoying herself—bridge, tennis, golf, garden clubs, and the like, while he finds no relief from work and, in fact, his life is quite the opposite. The further he goes, the greater the pressure becomes and the less opportunity he has to enjoy his success. It is at this point in their married life that mutual sensitivity is of paramount importance.

He must retain perspective on the forces operating on each. The responsibility is heaviest on him, for he is in the best position of the two to see both sides most clearly. He knows the pressures and responsibilities that he faces, and with very little imagination he can visualize her new life of freedom from raising the children and the opportunities he has provided through his financial success for her to enjoy herself.

She, on the other hand, is not in such a fortunate position, because she can never really understand the nature of the pressures and stress that are a part of his daily life. She can, however, recognize that although her life has changed markedly in terms of her growth of freedom, his has not, and she can pay attention to such things, for example, as death-rate statistics (published constantly in women's magazines, the daily newspaper, and other media), and draw the simple and obvious conclusions.

If, instead of being sensitive to what she is doing, however, she babbles and bubbles about her days of fun and games whenever they are together, he very likely will develop a jealousy that is very real, even if this is in conflict with his pride at having achieved the success that enables her to do all those things. Moreover, he may become suspicious of the people with whom she associates and suspect infidelity, even where none exists, even though common sense should tell him that their relationship would not permit this.

An eruption may occur when she complains about some silly frustration on a day that he has experienced a major disaster. The time from that point to an unhappy marriage or even divorce may be very short. An argument, once begun, may be hard to turn off, especially if it is aggravated by sexual denial, continued insensitivity ("He had no right to yell at me, I didn't do anything wrong!"), or an unfortunate separation for a time (a necessary business trip) during which self-righteous indignation can build to the unmanageable level of a Berlin wall where communication ceases.

This description, based on actual cases, can be further complicated by the fact that the middle-aged executive who is still working hard every day frequently sees women his wife's age—women who frequently are still working hard out of necessity. For example, when he works late at night, he sees a cleaning woman whose life of drudgery he can easily compare with that of his wife at home, living a life of comparative luxury. That emotion of identification and classification may, by itself, give rise to some negative feelings and nothing more. On the other hand, if he carries the same thought process into an identification with a female colleague who gives him any degree of encouragement, it is possible that an affair may result, with all of the obvious consequences.

f. *Resentment:* Surprisingly frequently, successful middle-agers harbor a good bit of resentment—another immature reaction that is focused on his subordinates, peers, supervisors, job, or family. Supporting his resentment is his growing awareness of the fragility of his position and the fears growing out of his rising vulnerability to the loss of everything he has worked so hard to obtain. (Fear and stress are very much a part of this entire problem.)

- He resents his subordinates, who often have learned in college what it took him many years of hard experience to acquire, and he sees them as threats to his position.
- He resents his peers, who, he believes, are enjoying their success and who have escaped (he thinks) the misery he feels.
- He resents his superiors, who (he believes) constantly raise their levels of expectations of him, always to unrealistic heights. (There may well be a high factual content to his perceptions which only further complicates the matter.)
- He resents his family, who are able to enjoy the material benefits of his success, while he must keep his nose to the grindstone, especially since he cannot communicate and share with them his insecurities and apprehensions.

The end result is an alienation of the individual from those whom he resents and strong guilt feelings over that resentment, creating an atmosphere charged with conflict potential.

2. Lack of a Meaningful Personal Philosophy. As is true of any event involving human behavior, no single factor can be described or identified as *the* underlying cause of the Mid-Life Crisis or even of mid-life problems in general. Indeed, the several or combination of causes in any one case are closely related to the makeup and life experiences of the individual and thus are, in large measure, unique.

On the other hand, from my experience, I have found that some causes are more commonly present than others, and it is possible that a few are universal.

In particular, if I had to focus on one single cause as being probably universal and of greatest significance, it would be the lack of a well-defined personal philosophy. The term *well-defined* is of critical importance. I do not suggest that a personal philosophy needs to be elaborate, complex, or lengthy, as one would associate with the philosophies of Aristotle, Spinoza, or Whitehead. Indeed, as a pragmatist, I believe that it must be suited to the needs of the individual who holds to the philosophy, and that means "all" of his needs, including those related to his ability to comprehend and willingness to attend to that philosophy.

The nature of the philosophy must, in keeping with the foregoing, be highly individualized and self-creative. In effect, the individual must create for himself a definition of the world (your world) and his role(s) in life (your roles in life) that will provide a reason for existing in the world and a means for handling the problems that he (you) experience throughout your lifetime.

For too many people, what passes for a personal philosophy is all wrapped up in a nice phrase that sounds good and sells plaques, bumper stickers, and softly-illustrated, very expensive books. Unfortunately, knowing that, "IF YOU ARE

NICE TO PEOPLE THEY WILL BE NICE TO YOU," doesn't help very much as a guide for your life when the doctor tells you that you have cancer and have only a 50-50 chance of surviving surgery.

Once you eliminate the problems of semantics and get through the defenses that are raised as a means of self protection, many middle-agers describe their lives in terms of "emptiness" and "loneliness," despite the fact of having been quite successful by the world's standards.

With specific reference to executives, there is an old cliche that it is "lonely at the top." The point of this statement is that the final and ultimate responsibility for the organization over which the individual exercises authority rests with the person in charge, be he a general, chief executive officer, or someone with similar powers.

In an entirely different sense, there is a true loneliness in far too many senior executives—a loneliness born out of the success they have achieved and identical with the loneliness felt by other middle-agers who, although not executives (be they factory workers or housewives), have reached a point in life where they can look back on a substantial number of years. What is seen at that point is that in the process of living, their sense of values has shifted to the point that accomplishment of goals (achievement no matter for what purpose) has become primary and everything else has been subordinated to it. Accordingly, emotion is often regarded as a sign of weakness, and self sufficiency becomes a major virtue.

A result of this transformation is that the individual loses his ability to empathize with others, and even worse, he loses touch with his own emotions. The final result, too frequently, is that the person is regarded with envy for being strong, decisive, able to help and guide others, truly the master of his fate and captain of his soul. On the other hand, the middle-ager at that point has few people (if anyone) he can talk to or with whom he can share his feelings.

Interestingly enough, some sort of tragedy can be very

beneficial in a situation of this sort. Divorce, loss of job, a major physical ailment, or anything else that brings the person up short and forces him to look at himself can also bring a realization of what has happened in his life and place him on a path of examining his values.

As I have spoken with executives over the past 25+ years, it is commonplace to find very successful men (and women) who are desperately seeking something of value which they have begun to realize has been lost along the way on their path to success. Some of the things that are examined in this search range from the extremes of formal religion to small local Bible study groups, to psychiatry, to the counsel of a good friend, to alcohol, to an extramarital affair, or to the joining of an extremist group operating on the lunatic fringe.

Man is by nature a gregarious creature who has a need to share himself emotionally with others. Indeed, he becomes whole as he is able to subordinate himself and his own desires to the service of others. A personal philosophy that does not take this into account will be ineffective.

Reduced to its simplest terms, everyone must face the fact that some day he will die. If he lives into old age he will experience, at best, an increasing degree of helplessness and dependency on others, and very likely along the way, the pain and suffering of one or more illnesses. Then, too, the universal complaint of all old people—loneliness—will be ever present. If the individual does not have something to hang onto—something outside of himself—something from which he can draw strength, from which he can find answers as to the reasons for his experiences and problems, something that will sustain him in moments of loss and tragedy, he will be a very (needlessly) unhappy person.

When I first began my formal study of the Mid-Life Crisis, despite my training as a psychologist, I was not prepared to find the lack of a personal philosophy to be such a universal problem. Once I accepted that fact, however, I next asked myself, "Why do so many people lack the inner strength that we, as a nation, have always prided ourselves in having in abundance?".

I am sure that there are as many answers to that question as there are people who would propose them, and, in the final analysis, I am also sure that there is no one or even a few answers that can cover every case. Yet, as I have studied the situation, one trail of circumstances describes a great many of the facts and I offer it here simply for consideration and the thoughts that it might provoke.

A simple study of history shows that men all over the world and at all times have devised some sort of religion to reconcile that vast gulf that exists between man's fragility on the one hand and the incomprehensible majesty and mysteries of nature on the other.

The advent of Christianity had a profound effect on the world, as did the religious revival known as the Reformation that occurred in the 1500s. At that point the Protestant church was born. Concomitant with the spread of the Reformation and its effects on man was the colonization of America. Following the American Revolution, waves of immigrants began to pour into this country, bringing with them two things:

> • A strong religious faith (personal philosophy) which had led to their persecution and immigration and which also provided them with the means for handling the problems of coming to a new country—as yet unsettled—and those attendant to moving west in a wilderness.
> • And hope—with or without a religious faith, the immigrants came to the United States with hope—hope that their lot would be better than it was in the old country and hope expressed in a conviction that not only would they be better off, but they would be able to obtain a far better life in all ways than was true in their native land. This too constitutes a form of a personal philosophy.

During the next 200 years, as the pioneers pushed west, the United States took on a basic character that was centered on the family as the basic unit of society, a family that built and went to church because its members believed in God. With hope, prosperity, and an expanding economy, our Judeo-Christian heritage became accepted as an institution in American society. With generally accepted standards of morality and belief, the tenents of Christianity and Judaism were accepted without challenge. Religion, going to church on Sunday, Sunday school, and the social role of the church were all tied closely to the positive character of the growing young nation. (An important feature here is that aspect of the character that was based upon the ever-expanding economy and ever-rising standard of living.)

Along the way, the real message of the church and the requirements for salvation (which everyone accepted as part of this "good" thing) were lost. It became a sort of a package deal: go to church and Sunday school, be good, and you will receive salvation. This concept is carried throughout many of our art forms. For example, in a large number of movies, a tough guy "sort of prays" while a bunch of other tough guys listen. He states that he "doesn't know much about this praying business," but he knows that he is being watched over by a supreme being who takes care of those whose hearts are good, even if they stray from the straight and narrow rather consistently. Then, in the great tradition of Hollywood, God saves them all from an impossible situation, and everyone lives happily ever after.

Those individuals who are today in or entering middle age, grew up under the influence of parents who had this "cotton candy" conception of religion. Very likely, they were given little or no training at home, but instead were sent to Sunday school for that education, and there were taught by other adults who also lacked a real understanding of what salvation requires.

Today, all too often, the middle-ager who needs something to lean on finds that he has nothing. His children call him a hypocrite because he proclaims one set of beliefs and yet practices another, while in vast numbers, they themselves do exactly the same thing.

As I noted earlier, man has always needed and still does need something outside of himself to lean on, to handle and explain life's traumas and problems that he cannot cope with himself. As the pioneers moved west, they found that strength in their society, and as society strengthened, the religion they held was watered down and weakened. Too many of the younger generation today (through grouping) have drawn strength from one another as teenagers. Sustaining one another, they have been able to avoid the responsibility of growing up and have resisted maturing as might otherwise have occurred on a natural basis.

The end result of all this is a generation (and now two generations) who lack any real kind of inner resources to sustain them when problems of living occur. For lack of a better term, I have called this inner resource a personal philosophy. If you wish, you can call it religion, religious faith, or just plain faith in God. Whatever you choose to call it, it is missing in too many of our churches, it is missing in too many of our institutions, and it is missing in too many who are middle-aged or younger. Hence, normal problems of living become crises.

3. Life's Options. As one grows older, an awareness develops that life's options and alternatives are narrowing and diminishing. This brings an increasing awareness of individual vulnerability and with it, usually a growing feeling of insecurity. The spectre of retirement and the end of one's career become visible. At this point, some people begin fighting the inevitability of reduced options. They give up a successful career and go into something else that may be entirely inappropriate—in an attempt, actually, to deny the fact of the aging process.

In this emotional state, the individual often develops a distorted view of his achievements and present position and becomes blinded to the satisfactions that exist in what he has, as opposed to what he thinks he can get or become. For example, the executive who gives up a successful career as a chief financial officer to join an archeological expedition in the Gobi desert has permitted his fantasies to overrule his judgment. The contrast in that situation is easy to see. On the other hand, how about the chief financial officer who at age 59 realizes that he cannot become president in his company and so resigns to become the controller of another organization where he is told that his future will be unlimited? By the time he becomes familiar with the business of his new employer, he will probably be 62 or 63, and I believe his chances to become president then will be much diminished.

Or, the middle-aged housewife who decides, "before I get too old," to get a job. Although she might be lucky, the chances are very high that she will end up in some menial occupation, the fatigue and frustration of which will probably negatively impact her marriage and family relationships.

Or, the highly skilled craftsman who figures that it is "now or never," and quits his job (leaving behind security, seniority, and the real satisfaction of making effective use of all of his accumulated skills and knowledge) to open his own business. In short order, he will probably find that operating even a very small business today requires that he spend very little time at the trade he so loves and long hours developing the business, doing paperwork, and complying with all types of regulations. Chances are also very good that he will be undercapitalized, and the statistics show that he will probably not make it.

The simple fact of life is that as one grows older, career options and alternatives *do* diminish. Properly viewed, however, such a realization can be placed easily in the "so what?" category.

4. Illness. Some few people are blessed with good health and rarely, if ever, must see a physician or take any type of medication. For the average middle-ager, however, there are many signs that health problems are real and must be regarded with some degree of respect. The more common signs include:

a. Friends and relatives are having strokes, heart attacks, surgery, and have to incorporate into their lives, medication for high blood pressure, diabetes, visual and auditory problems, and so on.

b. Friends and relatives are dying.

c. A cold which once could be basically ignored now requires time off of work, creates some panic and shock when inability to breathe wakes you up at night, and the cough that follows hangs on for four or five weeks.

d. Weight goes on and doesn't come off.

e. There is a considerably increased need for sleep and rest.

f. Dental problems become acute.

g. Cuts and bruises do not heal quickly or easily. Your physician tells you that it is time to begin having a physical examination at least once a year.

One of the major problems with illness in the middle years and beyond is that the symptoms rob the person of perspective. Rather than treating the immediate problem as transitory, the person is far more likely to develop a degree of depression in a symptom-related hysteria that makes concern for the present override every consideration for the future.

I have seen a self-confident, strong, aggressive, successful executive turned into a helpless, timorous, and enfeebled shadow of his former self by illness—all in a single week. The real problem is the resultant damage done to his image, self respect, and esteem in the eyes of his peers and supervisors when he recovers.

Psychosomatic illnesses also are found with increasing frequency in the middle years. As the spectre of serious illness becomes more real, ordinary aches and pains are blown out of all proportion, and cancer and cardiac arrest are seen lurking behind every twinge. (It is not unknown for many loving wives to drive their husbands up the wall with overconcern for health problems at this point in their lives.)

5. Frustration. This is an extremely broad problem. As people grow older, they begin to find more and more things that frustrate them. Parent-child relationships become an increasing source of conflict, and relationships with other people also create needs for adjustment.

One particularly knotty problem today is found in the area of values and the strong conflict of value systems that exists in our society. We find, for example, value systems in which there are fairly clear-cut differences between right and wrong—today's middle-agers grew up, by and large, in a society where these concepts predominated. At the same time, we find other value systems today where all is right and wrong is denied. Situational ethics, half values, and the concept of personal pleasure at the expense of others all exist simultaneously and produce emotional conflict of serious proportions.

Stress is an outgrowth of frustration (although it results from other things as well). When you work hard, relief begins the minute you stop, no matter how tired you are. Not so with stress. The pressure of stress does not end quickly, even when the stress-producing cause is eliminated. The effects (aftershock) hang on.

Thus stress is more debilitating than hard work. Unfortunately, it does not build up the muscles and thus has no positive consequences. Instead, its results are all negative on both the body and the mind. Coronary problems, stroke, high blood pressure, ulcers, bad temper, marital disharmony, and many other serious problems stem directly or in part from stress produced by frustration.

Stress is not limited to executives and professionals, even though those are the people to whom most articles on stress are pointed. It is a real problem for the blue-collar worker and for housewives, just as it is for those in positions of power where major decisions are required daily if not hourly.

The problem is that stress is the result of two interactive factors. The first is external and can be anything that is disruptive to the individual's life style, plans, goal pursuits, or normal activities. Such things can range from continuous disruptive noise when one is trying to concentrate all the way to a set of only partially controllable circumstances that could lead to the destruction of a career that has taken 20 years to build. The second factor is the personality of the individual. Some people will worry over anything, whereas others will remain calm and unruffled (inwardly) even under the most disruptive, chaotic, and ominous of situations. To complicate this even further, the same individual can react differentially to the same amount of a stress-producing cause, depending on the nature of that cause and on the total set of circumstances within which it occurs. Even further, a person's reactions vary in terms of cause, intensity and extent in different ways and different combinations at different times in his life. A man is not a static, unchanging being. Unfortunately, for far too many, the change in later years is toward a person who is frustrated by much and satisfied by little.

With specific respect to the Mid-Life Crisis, it is my observation that those who pass through the middle years most effectively generally have a well-developed personal philosophy of life that has at its core a substantive value system that will stand up firmly to all of the pressures placed against it.

6. A Feeling of Being Trapped. Although very much related to the fact that as one gets older, life's options and alternatives diminish, some special mention is required of the feeling of entrapment that many people experience with middle age.

Partly because of the realization that there isn't much time left to do the things he wants to do before he will be too old, partly because he is carrying a lot of responsibility that has been his to bear for a long period of time, and partly because he would like one last fling at being free and carefree, the middle-ager frequently feels that he is imprisoned in the cage of his life and, like any prisoner, he wants to escape.

Some middle-agers have a rather extreme reaction to the feeling of being trapped. The end result in these cases involves family desertions, separations and divorces, alcohol and drugs, extramarital affairs, and even depression and suicide. Much more commonly, however, the reaction is one of bitterness and cynicism, and the "sufferer" becomes hard to live with and his relationships with others become strained.

7. Emphasis on "Youth." One has only to turn on the television set or pick up any magazine to note by direct, blatant statement and by subtle inference that ours is a youth-oriented culture in which all things that are young, vibrant, alive, and happy are good, and everything that is old is bad.

Products sold from cosmetics to suppositories are intended to rejuvenate or put on the facade of youth. All the models used in advertising are young and have muscular, healthy bodies—frequently displayed with a great deal of bare flesh showing—the sort of thing that the not-young and not-muscular middle-ager tries to cover up and hide.

It would not be too much of an overstatement to say that Madison Avenue has created a mass inferiority complex for that portion of the population that is over 35.

The emphasis on youth, despite its commercial origins, is a mixed blessing. On the one hand, the results of the youth emphasis are positive to the extent that people are impelled by it to stay in (or return to) good physical condition and to maintain a constant vigilance over their state of health.

The negative consequences of the emphasis on youth are found in three areas:

a. Some people compare themselves negatively to the image of youth with which we are all surrounded and end up just feeling bad.

b. Some middle-agers feel that they can recapture their youth by changing their mode of dress, eating habits, and general behavior. Few things are more ridiculous looking than a man who is essentially bald except for a few straggly hairs and a fringe around his head that have been permitted to grow down to his collar, unless it is the middle-ager wearing clothes 30 years too young for him and risking a heart attack on the dance floor at a discotheque.

c. The worst consequence of all is found in the person (unfortunately, the vast majority of middle-agers) who in looking with reverence on youth—to the exclusion of all else—misses the joys and pleasures that youth cannot know and which are the exclusive province of those of middle age.

8. The Concept of Age. A major cause of the Mid-Life Crisis is a simple conditioned response to the concept of age.

Before he is able to talk, an infant is bombarded with commands and demands that he gauge his behavior and his thinking in terms of his chronological age, irrespective of even common-sense evidence to the contrary. From the very earliest days of his conscious awareness of such relationships, the child is taught that his chronological age dictates what he can and cannot do in most of his social relationships, what his status and qualifications are legally, and (unfortunately) how he should think, act and feel about himself, facts to the contrary not withstanding.

As a very young boy, the child is told:

- "You are too old to act like that."
- "You are not old enough yet to do that."
- "Big boys don't do that."
- "You have to go to school because you are 6 years old, that's why!"

This close tie between behavior and age is continued with legal enforcement. As the youngster grows, he gains legal status, including both privileges and responsibilities:

- At the age of 15 or 16, he can get working papers.
- Drivers' licenses are granted at various levels at various ages.
- At age 18, the young man assumes many legal rights and responsibilities.
- At age 21, he becomes totally, legally, free.

Along the way through adolescence there are social and religious ceremonies that mark points of achievement that are strictly related to age, irrespective of psychological, social, or physical development.

This concept is closely related to the concept of grouping and is a potent force in dictating many people's actions. For example, in recent years, the age of 30 has become a critical point. For many adolescents, those who are over 30 are "the enemy" who represent the establishment and whose hypocrisy must be defeated by the purity of the younger generation's ideals. "Age 30" or "Old Goat 40" parties are quite common— the concept here being that at that point in the person's life, they are ready for the scrap heap.

By the time middle age comes along, the individual is so conditioned that he does not need to stop or think about what he should do. Even though he may be in the best physical condition of his entire life, be fully mentally alert and highly creative, have great amounts of physical energy and strength, and be as sexually active as ever, he "knows" that none of these things *should* be. Accordingly, he "thinks himself" into mental and physical deterioration and begins that long process that eventually ends in senility and/or old age, long before either needs to be.

A great deal of research is needed in this area, but on the basis of my own professional experience and observations, I have no doubt whatsoever that the process of mental and physical deterioration can be slowed remarkably into very advanced ages.

The secret in this process is to avoid thinking of yourself

in terms of chronological age. Instead, look at yourself as you are today and totally ignore your age—as a factor in thinking about what you are, who you are, and what you are able to do.

For example, I know that I cannot do a lot of things—physically—that I was able to do 25 years ago. However, I do not dwell on that with regret, for those abilities were pertinent to that time, and that time is gone. Today, I am able to do what I am able to do and the kinds of skills, abilities, knowledge, and potentials that I have are different than they were 25 years ago, but also far greater in number.

9. Grouping. The concepts society has about age must be looked at from another standpoint. All the preceding factors, the subtle and the not so subtle, force the middle-ager into thinking of himself in terms of what "should happen" based on chronological age. Why should he be surprised, then (in the tradition of the Pygmalion effect), when it actually happens. The Bible and various philosophers have described the same concept with the phrase, "I think, therefore I am." However you describe it, it is simply an expression of the power of the mind over the body. Tell someone he is getting old, make him believe it, and it will happen.

If the middle-ager were merely "talked into" getting old as an individual, the problem would be bad enough. Even worse, however, is the fact that this kind of thinking results in:

a. Destroying the concept of individual differences.

b. Fostering the concept of grouping.

c. Setting up social barriers that force a person away from the very behavior that would not only be personally beneficial but would also avoid the Mid-Life Crisis and similar age-related problems in the first place.

It was not until the seventeenth and eighteenth centuries that the concept of grouping appeared. At that time childhood was recognized as a discernible period of life with special needs and characteristics. Adolescence is essentially a twentieth century invention, with "teenager" being a concept that grew out of World War II. Today, a special case is being made, slowly, for a new stage in life called youth. "Senior citizens" and now "middle-agers" are groups of even more recent vintage.

Unfortunately, although grouping is useful in focusing attention on the needs of various age groups and their particular characteristics, grouping really produces more negative than positive effects. For example, not long ago there was no such thing as a teenager. Adolescence moved from childhood to adulthood, during which process the young person experienced physiological and emotional changes that, when faced up to, were generally dispensed with readily.

Under the grouping concept, the cliche that, "misery loves company," comes to its worst realization. A shared misery is usually prolonged and regarded as more acceptable than something one must face alone and overcome. Thus the concept of the teenager has emphasized and made the adjustment problems of moving into adulthood a mass problem that it is acceptable to avoid by any available means. During the 1960s, we had a graphic example of almost an entire generation that rebelled against taking on the responsibilities that accompanied their legal and physiological growth.

In the same manner, rather than face up to a problem and attempt to solve it, it is far easier for a middle-aged person to say, "Well, everyone has these troubles, so I guess I can just live with them."

It is a simple fact of life that people adapt readily and quickly in both behavior and thinking to the group with which they identify. The adopted behavior and thinking are generally blind, ignorant, and mindless adherence to the stereotypes set and considered a part of the group. In addition, the avoidance of reality is furthered by intragroup pressure and by advertising. For example, parents (one age group) stress the concept of "teenager" and foster all the marks and signs of teenager identification such as clothing, use of the teenager label, and (worst of all) acceptance of stereotyped behavior as "normal." Further, advertisers play on the teenage concept to sell products (positive approach), and on middle-agers to sell products that will help them not look like middle-agers (negative approach by emphasizing the youth culture again). Whichever direction is being taken, the end result—group identification and solidarity—is furthered and reality is obscured.

Going one last step, as group identification grows, so too does peer pressure. Even one generation ago, peer pressure was far weaker than it is today, even though it has always had some effect. As individuality and thinking have slipped, moral values have also disappeared, behavior has become stereotyped (it is acceptable to do what the group approves of), and the cycle that further strengthens the group continues.

My personal philosophy is that chronological age is not a meaningful index of anything. Rather, middle age is a state of mind, the avoidance or denial of which can eliminate many of the problems being described here as part of the Mid-Life Crisis. I thus reject the concept of grouping and, instead, think of life as a continuous process. Even though physiological aging occurs and cannot be ignored, there are compensating abilities, advantages, and benefits at every age that are not available at any other. With this concept, the future holds as many new challenges and opportunities as was true for all prior stages.

One final point: it is an unfortunate fact of life that good and bad are frequently wrapped up together in the same circumstances, and this is particularly true in one aspect of the grouping concept. In recent years, "senior citizens" have been identified as a group, special clubs have been formed, and special privileges have been accorded to people who fit into that age range. Basically, this is very good, and I am fully in support of these matters. In particular, I support the benefit that accrues to senior citizens who, facing the major enemy of old age—loneliness—find emotional support and kinship and belonging with others who are also old. On the other hand, although senior citizen clubs provide a lot of good times for older people, the whole purpose of the label, the clubs, and the benefits is a reaction to the negative attitudes toward old age that so many people have. It would be far better for older people to forget age completely and live their lives at the point they have reached. It would still be possible to have the clubs and the privileges, but as a positive thing, not as a reaction to something that is negative. The point may be a fine one, but I believe it is important.

10. Depth of Personal Relationships. Many individuals in our society are so involved with "things" and so over involved with so many "different things" that they have little opportunity to develop close interpersonal relationships with very many people.

The loneliness mentioned previously frequently begins to evidence itself during the middle years, as friends and relatives begin to die off, children grow up and move away, and close working associates retire (usually to someplace else, since no one seems to ever be satisfied to be where they are).

For many couples, mid-life is a time in their marriage when they have begun to take one another for granted. Problems result when:

• They don't recognize what has happened.
• They do recognize it but won't, or feel they can't do anything about it.
• Other problems combine with this one, such as the desire to *prove* that youth is not over.

Man is by nature a gregarious creature, and without friends with whom he can share his emotions, he is both incomplete and unable to find true expression of himself.

Establishing close personal relationships with other people is very tricky. With an increasingly mobile society, it is becoming more and more common for close friends and neighbors to pack up and move halfway across the country on almost a moment's notice. As I write these words, the memory of a party my wife and I attended last night is still fresh. Close friends, who moved away several years ago, returned for one day, and we got together with a number of other friends to renew acquaintances. It was a happy occasion. However, it was also very very clear that although personal feelings between us all are close and strong, the support and strength that come from day-to-day contact and physical presence "when needed" was missing, and probably will never be there again.

Again, because everyone seems to be flying off in all directions at the same time, it is possible for people to live next door to each other as neighbors for many years and never really get to know one another. The problem, then, is a real one, and it cannot be corrected without direct and deliberate attention.

Finally, good interpersonal relationships require a good self image. You can't build on a poor base. Again—the causes are interrelated.

11. Fears. The fact of fear is becoming more and more of a problem for more and more middle-agers. In fact, as my conversations with those in the middle years become more extensive and include an ever-widening sphere of people, fear of one thing or another and of one sort or another seems to be a constant and growing problem.

   a. *Fear Related to the Pressure of Deadlines:* Bills to be paid, people to be faced, questions to be asked, answers to be readied, reports to be completed, and arrangements to be set.

   b. *Fear Born Out of Living in a Rat Race:* Needed repairs on the house, income less than outgo, kids still to go to college, working more hours than you want to, and worse, working more hours than you need to, running out of money at the counter and being fearful of bringing that news home.

c. *Fear that Is Brought on by Giving up of Ourselves:* The denial of our personhood and family responsibilities, neglecting children for the sake of survival, not sharing the realities of the pressures of work with your wife (or husband) all of the time, those responsibilities and pressures straining the relationship even to the point of estrangement, afraid to say, "Hey, I can't make it alone, I need help."

d. *Fear of Failure:* Of losing all you have earned and won by years of toil.

e. *The Fear of Illness:* Of death, of suffering, of getting old, of being a burden, of having no more friends and having no one.

f. *The Fear of the End Coming Too Soon:* Not being ready for it, of the end being just that—only an end.

g. *The Fear of Being Honest and Standing Up for What You Believe:* Afraid of what others might think, not sure of what they think, of the consequences, and of loss of self respect if you don't speak up.

h. *Fear of Old Age:* Because our society views old age as a disaster, of being feeble, useless parasites who are nothing better than a drag on society.

i. *Fear of Being Fired:* Mid-life desperation also results from the fear of being fired. Many businesses and other organizations have as strong an emphasis on youth as does the world of advertising. When a man has only a few years left until retirement and begins to see himself blocked from further advancement by his age, while being expected to continue to produce at the same rate as ever if not increase that rate, his fear of being fired increases and frequently reaches the point of panic. Intelligent management could well provide him with security and an opportunity to make full use of his skills, while at the same time, the opportunity to slow down somewhat before eventual retirement. All too often, that intelligent management is lacking.

j. *Fear Born Out of Pressure:* As redundant as it may be, pressure and stress are a problem that often lead to fear and other emotions that are closely related to it. For example:

• *Fear:* job loss, illness, death, being a victim of crime, war, and so on.

• *Anger:* high taxes, government waste, newspaper stories of elected officials on junkets, elected officials who support family members on government payrolls (family members who frequently don't work), elected officials who hire girl friends who can't type or answer the phone, criminals released due to technicalities, soft judges, increasing law violations infringing his rights, and so on.
• *Frustration:* a constant stream of little rip-offs and no way to obtain justice or simple satisfaction.

Fear + anger + frustration = pressure. The pressure slowly builds until it boils over into other phases of the middle-ager's life. This is true for everyone, of course, but the middle-ager is more sensitive to it because of the other causes listed in this chapter, and thus he has a lower tolerance level.

We are a desperate people—pressured and drained and battered and plagued and depressed and lonely.

There are those who will say that the foregoing is overly dramatic, unreal, and contrary to the facts. To those I would answer, take a look at the facts! Take a look at the incidence of drug addiction, alcoholism, suicide, divorce, desertion, antisocial behavior, wife beating and child abuse—by middle-agers—then try to tell me that it is overly dramatic.

12. Fear of Death. As a precipitating cause of the Mid-Life Crisis this is such a special fear that it requires special attention.

Most people come face-to-face with the reality of death three times in their lives. First, somewhere in the early years of life (for me it happened at age 7) the individual learns that life will end in death. For most, that passes very quickly. (I cried myself to sleep that night and the next day promptly forgot about the whole thing.)

Second, somewhere in the middle years, death again becomes a reality. Faced with that reality, most people reject it. Somewhere recently I read that 85% of all the people who die in the United States do so without leaving a will. Whether or not that statistic is accurate, one thing is obvious: in a society geared to the veneration of youth, physical strength, and sex-ual virility, people react negatively when threatened with the loss of these things.

As this is being written, courts of law are struggling with the concept of how much effort should be made to sustain life, since at the present time there is no limit on the efforts that we can make to prevent death. Also, for the first time, after people have died by the millions for thousands of years, we have come to the realization that we don't really know what death is, and so it is being studied. The end result of that research will have important social, legal, moral, and personal consequences.

What is behind all of this?

a. There is an increase in the reality of death for most people. Because of television, the atomic bomb, and the communication explosion, it is rare to go through a day without seeing a picture of a dead person or to hear about an event somewhere on the face of the earth that does not have some possible impact on our own potentiality for survival. Also, as religion has come to mean less and less for more and more people, death takes on a finality that it does not have for those who believe in eternal life; thus death is something that must be pushed off as far as possible, for with it comes indeed the end.

b. During the past few years there has been a growth in irrational thoughts concerning life and death. Throughout history, most people have shown a strong desire to either live forever (in some form) or at the very least to not at the end pass into nothingness and be forgotten. As people have rejected what have generally been regarded as the true religions (the rejection, interestingly enough, having come about largely through ignorance of what was being rejected), support is sought through dependence on other externals such as alcohol, drugs, social groups, and many others that again can only be described as the lunatic fringe.

With the growing awareness of death as a future reality, many middle-aged men develop the desire (goal) of being able to look back from their deathbed, so to speak, and view their life as having been important and worthwhile. The desire to have accomplished something or to at least have tried to accomplish something becomes very strong. Recognizing that death will come and seeing retirement as an event in the relatively near future, they experience a growing sense of urgency, almost desperation, to reach the goal of having accomplished something that will satisfy their felt need. This desperation frequently leads to an intensification of personal effort that may well bring additional success to the man but have negative consequences on his family.

Some difficult-to-understand behavior can be seen in the fact that most people do not associate death with themselves even when face to face with it, such as at a funeral or wake. Man has the capability of insulating himself from the reality of such situations, even while feeling the emotion of grief and personal loss at the death of a friend or close relative.

Finally, the last face-to-face encounter with death is when one actually reaches that point in his own life. Then, surprisingly enough, it is frequently still denied even as it is happening. Most people simply are unable to cope with the concept of dying and reject it to the very end. There is little wonder that it creates the problems that it does such as a Mid-Life Crisis.

SUMMARY

In conclusion, the causes of a Mid-Life Crisis and mid-life problems are many and varied. More importantly, those for any one individual are probably unique, and any lengthy listing of possible causes can only be academic.

Most of what has been said thus far has been negative and probably depressing. All of the foregoing has only served to set the stage.

Mid-Life Crises can be avoided or solved.

You can do a great deal to help yourself without buying anything or taking any remedies.

Read on.

5 How to Solve Mid-Life Problems

(Or, How to Avoid Them in the First Place)

The process involved in and required for avoiding or solving mid-life problems is basically quite simple. Making it happen is not that easy.

The problem is that *anyone* can do the things that need to be done, both preventative and/or remedial, but it takes time, effort, and willingness. For whatever reason, not everyone is capable or willing of such a commitment.

Perhaps it is human nature that most people will not act to avoid potential problems, especially in matters wherein they feel themselves to have some control of the situation. Usually, they wait until a crisis occurs. Maybe it is that people are born gamblers and are willing to take a chance, even when their own happiness is at stake, and they are playing with the welfare and happiness of others whom they claim to love.

In the case of the Mid-Life Crisis, acting to resolve an existing problem *can* usually prove successful, even though it is far simpler and easier to avoid the problem while it is still in the "potential" stage. Since most mid-life problems are "potential" for every human being today, it stands to reason that preventative measures also need to be taken by everyone.

In my opinion, mid-life problems and the potential of their occurring truly provide everyone with the concept of a crisis that embodies elements of both danger and opportunity. The *danger* lies either in failing to avoid the potential problem in the first place or failing to act once it has occurred. The *opportunity* is found in the incentive that the potential or real problem can provide to impell actions that will result in greater personal happiness, the avoidance of unhappiness, and the gaining of the many satisfactions that emanate from a purposeful life.

There was a time in my career that I believed people fully when they said to me, "Please help me solve this problem, I really want to get rid of it," or, "I will do anything to provide for the happiness and welfare of my family." In far too many cases, when I have heard that declaration of distress, the lack of action that followed proved beyond a shadow of a doubt that they were not serious.

I have absolute conviction that you can avoid a crisis and/or prevent or solve almost any mid-life problem. To do so, however, you

- Must really want to do so.
- Must prefer being happy to being unhappy.
- Must be willing to work at it. (There are no magic pills, and it will not happen by itself.)

The *real* strength of your desire for happiness is just about the only criterion of whether or not it will happen. If you want to live a better life, you can! If you want to avoid problems (that are avoidable), you can! If you want your family to be happier, they can be! If you want to achieve all that you possibly can with your abilities, it can happen!

The program involves 10 steps.

Step #1: Stop thinking of age and of being part of an age group!

You are yourself! You are living a life that had a beginning and will have an end. In between, every age is as good as every other age, and all age periods are different. Most people fear growing old. Yet, the little evidence we have is beginning to show that old age is probably as much a state of mind as it is a physiological condition. (Obviously, I am not talking about the individual who suffers a major physiological calamity such as cancer, a stroke, crippling arthritis, or similar problems. But even with those there is a good bit of hope.)

The main point is that a mature understanding of one's own life is an essential ingredient in getting the most out of that life. Looking forward to death either as an escape or with a fear that dominates one's thinking is abnormal. Accepting death as a normal event is mature. There is an old saying that goes something like this, "Nature brings us into this world and teaches us how to live. Then, in her infinite wisdom, she shows us how to die." Most people who are able to face the facts of life get a great deal more out of it than those who don't.

The average person spends almost all his life in preparation for something that is going to occur later on. The focus of today's thought and effort is for tomorrow's benefit, but somehow, when tomorrow arrives, the process will be repeated.

I have often said that the ideal age in life is age 3, for at that point the child usually can talk, is able to get around quite well, and lives almost totally for the moment. After that, it's all down hill:

• Grammar school students look forward to the joys and freedom of being in high school.
• High schoolers prepare for and look to college as a time of freedom and enjoyment.
• College students look forward to and prepare for a career.
• Those who are beginning a career look forward to success and advancement.
• In mid-life, the goal is a happy retirement.
• At retirement, planning is done and sights are set on making sure that you can get along as long as you live, *or* the future is viewed with dread.

Far too many people spend the bulk of their lives looking forward to the freedom of retirement when they can travel, relax, and enjoy themselves, only to find that once retirement arrives, their dreams cannot be realized because they are too old, too poor, too ill, or too dead.

There is absolutely *nothing* wrong with planning for the future—in fact, planning is an essential ingredient to a happy life. However, if by looking forward, today is lost, then nothing really is gained.

Every stage and age of life has its potential joys as well as its all-too-real problems. More often than not, the problems get in the way of the potential joys, or the possibilities for happiness are pushed aside by setting your sights on the future as a time when you will begin to enjoy yourself and viewing today as a time to be endured in preparation for that eventual happiness.

Unfortunately, it is the rare person who ever arrives at the point where there will not be problems competing with the potentiality for immediate happiness. At the same time, I frequently hear expressions of regret for times that are passed which can never be recaptured, when joy was missed. A frequent example of this is found with middle-agers who found the problems of raising children prevented them from enjoying their children. Now, they look back and wish, with great regret, that they had lived those years for what they were really worth. The happy event of going away to college is a major tragedy for too many parents simply because of their own guilt feelings.

In the final analysis, the answer is that unless one is willing to look for enjoyment in one's life as it is today, future pleasures will be impacted negatively by regrets for joys that were missed at an earlier time.

So, for all these reasons and all of those listed in Chapter 4, *forget age!!!*

With all the money in the world you can't change one

minute or even one second of what has happened in the past. On the other hand, you can do a great deal to control what will happen in the future. Most of all, you can *live today* so that the effect on tomorrow will be positive.

• Enjoy today—forget the past (in terms of its negatives or regrets).
• Plan for tomorrow as though it will be the happiest, fullest time of your life. (Make the Pygmalion effect work for you.)
• Stress today and tomorrow so much in your mind that when someone asks you how old you are, you have to dig out your birth certificate to find out.
• Get to the point that when your age "group" is mentioned, you think of "them" as apart from yourself without any sense of identification with them.

You can do it—if you try hard enough!

Step #2: Accept the fact that a Mid-life Crisis can happen (or has happened) and make up your mind to do something about it!

That conviction is essential! . . . Without it, you will not act!

There is no point or purpose in my rambling on about this! Make up your mind right now! Either you're going to do something about the problem or you're not. If you're not, stop reading, close the book, and get back on your treadmill.

Better yet, don't just put this book down or throw it away, give it to someone with better sense than you have. They will probably find it to be of help.

Step #3: Take control of your own life.

Very few people really control their own lives. Most of the executives I have talked to over the past 25 years have reached
their present positions more by chance than by directed,
planned action. Someone else aided them, moved them along,
or prodded them into the action or place that resulted in their
current achievement.

Most of the people that I have met (and because of my
work I meet hundreds of people every year, many of whom
tell me about their life histories in great detail) have arrived at
their present point in life not by design or plan, but rather by
reaction to circumstances, accident, or sheer chance. (Incidentally, most people won't admit that fact, but it is true.)

Beyond the vagaries of history, how much control do you
exercise over your life today? Of the things that you do, how
many do you do because *you* want to and how many are you
involved in because someone else has pushed you into it, told
you that you "have to do it," or has made you feel guilty if you
don't?

Do you really enjoy doing all the things you are involved
in? Are you productive in those things that you don't like? Are
you really doing anything at all that is worthwhile?

One man that I know recently found himself in the following situation: he receives a great deal of satisfaction out of
helping other people and has great difficulty saying "no."
When I suggested that he take control of his life, he looked
at himself and found that he was involved in the work of about
twelve different organizations; he had too little time to do
anything of substance in any one of those organizations; his
phone rang constantly with demands from one or another of
the organizations—demands that he could not meet—he constantly felt guilty because of his lack of performance; the work
that he did do he was ashamed of because he knew that given

adequate time and opportunity he could do much better, and the entire affair had begun to affect his professional career. Over a relatively short period of time, he reduced the number of organizations he was involved in to two. He still has difficulty saying "no," but he is learning to do this, and in the time available, he is making substantial and significant contributions to the two organizations with which he is involved. His phone doesn't ring nearly as often, his career is back in balance, and he is far happier.

What I am suggesting here is nothing more complicated than merely "putting your house in order" by taking a look at the things you do and equating the time you spend on them with the returns received in terms of personal satisfaction, enjoyment, and productivity.

In another sense, I'm suggesting that you put your various activities and facets of your life into perspective, for some of the things I am going to suggest below will take some time, and time is a precious commodity.

In taking stock of your life, you will need to be objective and honest. These are two very difficult qualities to acquire. Unfortunately, although we judge other people by their behavior, we judge ourselves by our intentions, and in that manner excuse ourselves for our failures and are able to rationalize away laziness, immature behavior, and stupidity.

For example, for many years I have heard people claim that their jobs occupy so much of their time that they have no time for their families. To help me gain some sort of perspective on that point, I conducted a small survey in which I asked people to give me a fairly accurate accounting of the time they spent at home, on the job, and in other activities. The time spent at home, on the average, was pretty much in proportion and balance to what most people might consider as proper. On the other hand, in those hours at home, far too great a proportion of the time was spent reading the newspaper, watching television, doing work brought home from the office, working around the house (alone), and in sleep.

Thus when you look at your activities, be honest with yourself.

This point is so important as preparation for the next two points that I would like to summarize what I have said. In essence it is, get your life in order—now and first. Take a look at what you are doing with your life. Evaluate the worth of each of the aspects of it. Drop those things that have no value. Spend time on those things that do have value. Place the emphasis where the end result will be genuine happiness, not hedonistic pleasure. Make room for a positive, fulfilling future and aim toward personal growth. The difference between true happiness and hedonism is critical here. Doing something just because "it feels good," as a way of life, is particularly ridiculous. True happiness is far more complicated and satisfying than that.

For most people, happiness involves a great deal that is outside of "the self" and is in large measure unselfish. Unfortunately, that fact is something you can never understand until you try it, and even then you have to get used to it before you can appreciate what you have. At one and the same time, true happiness is deeply satisfying, all-encompassing, and fragile.

Step #4: Self-Evaluation

The reason you must take control of your life first, before going on, is that there are certain basic things that you must do (work for a living, sleep, eat, etc.) and many many others in which you have the option and choice. Control here is easiest to exercise, and from doing it you can learn a great deal. For example, you can learn that other people do exert a major influence on your life, and the experience of dealing with that will help you take the next step. As a specific case in point, I recently made the decision to stop drinking alcohol, in any form, totally. My many friends and acquaintances know that I have over the years had a drink occasionally and that my total consumption has been modest at best. Now that I have stopped, however, the pressure to have a drink is unbelievably strong; to retain friendships has required tact and diplomacy, and the firmness of my resolution has been tested strongly. It is clear that many people harbor strong guilt feelings about their drinking and are uncomfortable in the presence of someone who does not join them. It is also clear that the myths and social customs surrounding drinking are so deeply embedded in our culture that to want to do otherwise is regarded with suspicion and even hostility.

Moving on to a deeper level, the next step in the process is to determine what the raw materials you have to work with in setting up a game plan for the rest of your life are. To do this requires self-evaluation, and herein, again, lies another problem.

If asked, almost everyone would state that he evaluates himself and his life constantly. In fact, this is simply not true. During the past 30 years I have interviewed thousands of people of all ages and stations in life. Self-evaluation is so rare as to be almost nonexistent, recognizing that I am talking about *true* self-evaluation and not merely a passing superficial appraisal.

As human beings, we excuse our failures by judging our intentions rather than our behavior; we make myriads of assumptions about what we can or will do; and we gloss over impossible problems with solutions that, examined in the light of day, are nothing but daydreams.

Because of the foregoing, any true self-evaluation must be reduced to writing and, preferably, evaluated by someone else. (See Step #9 below.) If you can do this and overcome your natural defensiveness when your fancies are separated from facts, the end result will be highly satisfying and productive. If you are not strong enough to do that, then you might just as well go on living in the dream world you have constructed for yourself and accept the fact that you are going to be very unhappy for the most of the rest of your life and that your life will have about as much value as a stone.

There is a very strong assumption here that can prove troublesome unless you are willing to face it with some degree of maturity. The end result of a self-evaluation is that once you have an accurate picture of yourself, you have to be able to accept yourself as you are. Once you do so, you are on a good basis for moving forward, but until you do so, you are only kidding yourself.

It is extremely important to realize that you, like your fingerprints, are different from those of any other person who has ever lived or ever will live. Because of that fact, you have a unique contribution to make to this world, one that only you can make. Therefore, why try to be something you are not? Why not be about what you are really well-equipped to be, learn how to maximize and do that thing for which you are uniquely qualified, and make your mark in the world in terms of the things that are the natural outgrowth of your abilities, talents, and interests.

Before going on, I believe it is crucial to make the point that all I am suggesting to be done should be done in writing. People who "think things through" play mental leap frog, skip around, ignore facts, make unfounded assumptions, and, in general, play games. By reducing what you are thinking to writing, you are forced to face up to the fact of what you are doing, and you are much more likely to produce an end result that is valid and useful.

At exactly the same time, it is equally important to keep your written project as simple as possible. If it becomes overly complex or involved, you simply won't do it; thus a fine balance must be drawn between the two. In the last few years I have seen a number of systems involving printed forms on which you list your strengths, weaknesses, goals, and so on. I perfer something far simpler than that, something that focuses on the ultimate objective you are attempting to achieve—namely, what should you do with your life and how can you best do it?

You can look at your life two ways, externally or internally. Most people do one or the other, some do a little of both.

Externally: Life is measurable in terms of success or achievement. Emphasis is usually on:

- Financial status.
- Being able to send your children to college—a "good" college.
- Eating steak rather than hot dogs.
- Being well liked by your children.
- Being well off.
- Providing opportunities for your children you never had.
- Achieving goals.
- Things that you can "own" or "do."
- Being a good parent by being actively involved in all that your children do.

Internally: Life is not measurable in quantitative terms. Emphasis is on:

- The quality of life.
- Service to others.
- Attitudes.
- Your strengths and weaknesses.
- Your relationship with God.
- Personal growth as a human being.
- Your developmental needs.

Contrary to popular belief, the "internals" *do not* exclude the "externals." The problem is one of what receives *primary* emphasis and what flows *from* what.

Internal values cannot grow out of or be stimulated by the external values. The reverse, however, can and usually does happen.

The person who emphasizes internal values does not have to be (and if he is for real will not be) a dreamy-eyed drifter. Emphasis on the enduring values of life does not preclude using your God-given talents fully. Indeed, it would be impossible to be concerned with service to others (for example) and not develop as completely as possible all of your talents, abilities, and potential. To do otherwise is to place yourself above your creator—he gave you your aptitudes—for you to fail to make use of them is to declare that He was wrong.

For your self-analysis, you should include the following:

Self-Analysis

1. *What is your basic purpose in life?* (Why are you on earth, what do you hope to achieve with your life, and what do you want to be remembered for?)

2. *What are the things that are really and truly important to you?* (This question is asking you what your values are, and it may well take a little while for you to assemble a list of those things that really are important to you. Here, your values and not those of the rest of the world are what is important.)

3. *What are the practical considerations that have to be considered for the rest of your life?* (Include here such things as what you *have* to do, whether you want to or not, such as earn a living, raise a child for the next six or seven years until he is able to care for himself, etc. Include everything that is involved—for example, if you have to earn a living for yourself, what is the minimum amount of money you must earn to maintain the life style you feel is basically essential and without which you cannot exist?)

4. *What are your greatest strengths?* (Keep your list fairly short—no more than 10 items—but refine it to include all of the important ones, in rank order.)

5. *What are your strongest and most limiting shortcomings (mental, physical, etc.)?* (Once again, keep your list to no more than 10 items.)

6. *What are those things that you most enjoy doing and do*

best? (Again, keep your list short.)

7. *What are those things you dislike to do and/or do not do well?* (Include all you can think of.)

8. *What are those things that you* will *do?* (Perhaps for some people it would be better to list those things that you *will not* do, for whatever reason.) Here is a real test of your objectivity and honesty with yourself!

9. *What major advantages do you have, such as financial independence, freedom to move about as you wish, and so on?*

The end product of this procedure will be used in Step #7 below.

Step #5: Examine your personal philosophy of life.

Everyone has some idea about life and his place in it. Far too few people, however, have really come to grips with this matter, at least to the point of gaining a clear picture of what it is they believe in and beyond that point to one of using those beliefs as guides for their lives.

To recap some of the things I have said previously, our society has undergone profound change since the end of World War II. Many people have experienced a growth of freedom, but often at the expense of the freedom of others. The rate of our technological and cultural change, as noted earlier, has accelerated to such a point that we are just about incapable of changing further with it. Drug addiction has become a source of national shame, and addicts range from newborns to those who are on the verge of death from old age. Alcoholism is found in 1 out of every 20 people—men, women, and children. (Recently released figures show that one out of every four 13 year olds uses alcohol to some extent.)

Violent crimes have reached the point that most people

fear to walk the streets at night, and all of our lives have been affected to some extent, even in our own homes. The sale of guard dogs, burglar alarm systems, and door locks testifies to that fact.

Personal standards and moral values have fallen so far that it is almost impossible to watch television, and fully impossible to go to a movie, without seeing and hearing things that, only a few years ago, would have been offensive to even the most liberal-minded person and would not have been permitted by local authorities. The distinction between right and wrong used to be relatively easy, because your immediate society shared your values and you drew strength from that fact. Today, you probably must stand alone, and that is difficult, especially if you don't have a well-defined value system of your own that you are willing to defend—and, believe me, you *will* have to defend it.

Fewer and fewer people can handle the concept of sin. More and more people meet this problem by adopting and following a value system that accepts almost anything. Thus because they are not "committing" a sin, they have no problem of guilt feelings. The children of these people, however, go through their teen years and reach adulthood without the benefit of moral guidelines or concepts. Very recently, I attended a high school graduation ceremony and what I observed there convinced me beyond the shadow of a doubt that unless something is done soon, our society can and probably will break down completely.

Thus the first question you must ask yourself is, "What are my values?", that is, what are the things that are most important to me? As noted earlier, there are many moral value systems in our society—but what is your system? What do you believe in? What is right and wrong for you? Let's assume that you are 55 years of age and can look forward to 20 more years of life. What would you like to accomplish in that time? Would you like to be remembered for some contribution to the world?

Do you want to just enjoy yourself? Do you want to help other people (in general or in terms of specific individuals)? In other words, what is your purpose in living? Why were "you" put on this earth? A little introspective thought on this subject will make much clearer the actions you need to take to accomplish your objectives.

Similarly, how well prepared are you to meet the crises you must some day face: loss of friends and relatives, illnesses, and even your own eventual death? This is a problem that you must solve for yourself, even though help is available.

If you don't have a meaningful personal philosophy, don't despair. There are many value systems to choose from today. They can and will promise to fill any need. Most of them are worthless; their prophets are charlatans. Most "homemade" or "lunatic-fringe" new-style philosophy has little value or meaning. In choosing what to believe, select carefully so that your needs can best be met when a crisis occurs.

Finding answers to the questions I have listed and the many more that you have or will have and selecting your value system are not easy tasks. People in executive positions and those in the service professions will have a particularly difficult time in this regard. The professional life style of these individuals is oriented toward thinking outwardly in the solution of problems and in dealing with the problems of others. To look inwardly, in a type of self-analysis, is very difficult.

From the standpoint of overcoming a Mid-Life Crisis, or in preventing it in the first place or making it into a positive thing, relatively little of permanence can be accomplished unless you have a well-defined personal philosophy or a well-founded moral value system to serve as a foundation. Indeed, the lack of a well-developed personal philosophy is a prime cause of many Mid-Life Crises for many people and also a major roadblock to the resolution of the problem once it has come into being.

People involved in civil rights, women's liberation, youth,

and many other "causes," tell us what we should believe. We find ourselves, in the middle years, caught between the values of our parents and those of our children. Despite all attempts to train our children in one way, we find that the pressures of their peer groups are so strong and their inner resources are so weak that they openly accept beliefs contrary to our own and precepts far different from those that we try to teach them. We also find that morality is becoming a matter of law rather than personal conviction. In the face of all of this, it is not surprising that the middle-ager has trouble finding and hanging onto something of value.

For me, the answer is faith in Jesus Christ. For you, it may be something else. Whatever it is, it must be a belief in something that can serve as a foundation strong enough to sustain you in times of severe strain, something that is consistent.

To cope with life and its many problems, one needs a means of self-orientation. Whatever that means may be, such guidance is essential to a well-balanced life. You have a simple choice: you can lead an ethical life or you can lead an unethical life. You can't have it both ways.

Before going on, it will be helpful to you to think for a moment about the reasons for going through this exercise in the first place. Why does one need a personal philosophy? To help answer this question consider the following:

Purpose of a Personal Philosophy

If man were in complete charge of his life, destiny, and world (in other words if he were God), he would need nothing more. Unfortunately, man is human; in comparison to nature he is weak and very fallible, and he is often confused by the events that occur to and around him. Moreover:

1. People need a purpose in life if they are to:
    - Get the most out of it.
    - Make sense out of all the problems and pain of life.

• Achieve the best of which they are capable (self-actualization).

2. A personal philosophy provides a set of guidelines for living (very much like company policies):

• If you are inconsistent in what you do, you won't make sense to yourself.
• If you are inconsistent in what you do, people very likely won't trust you, and you will find yourself all alone.

3. A personal philosophy in mid-life:

• Will provide a means of retaining stability when major problems erupt.
• Will provide a solid anchor point when everything else becomes a tower of jello.
• Will enable you to fit together into some sort of rational explanation of the events of your life that will appear to be in strong conflict.
• Will keep a Mid-Life Crisis from happening.

I could spend the next 20 pages giving examples of the floundering people do who have not put together any type of rational philosophy that helps them to make sense out of their lives, but little purpose would be served, and it would be highly repetitious. Instead, let me cite only a few examples:

1. Your daughter comes home from college to tell you that she is living with a young man (to whom she is not married) and that they are about to have a child. You can neither understand nor explain this, since she has always been a "good" girl who never disobeyed you and always was a leader in her Sunday school class.

2. You wake up one morning and find that you and your wife are on different wave lengths. She has built a life totally separate from yours. With the children gone, you now must live more closely together than ever before, and you find that you have very little in common. Your task is to build a new relationship out of an old one, and you find that you have nothing to build it on.

3. You retire and find yourself all day long in the company of your wife. You get on each other's nerves because you don't have a meaningful relationship.

4. Six months ago you lost your job and have no realistic prospects of finding another one. The emotional impact of this has been visible to others for some time, and now even you become aware of the fact that you are drinking too much, sitting and brooding rather than actively pursuing job leads, and have become a royal pain in the neck to everyone you know.

5. Tragedy has happened—you have retired—and you begin the slow process of deterioration that can have only one end.

6. A close relative (wife, child, parent, sibling, etc.) dies.

All of these and more are the province of the middle-ager. To those who have some way of making sense out of it all there is a proper balance of emotions, but these normal events do not destroy the person or at best result in a negative change in their outlook or behavior.

Let's suppose that you don't have a philosophy of life. You have two choices. You can either adopt one that is already in existence, or you can build one from scratch. Building a philosophy of life from scratch is much too complicated a task to be realistic for any but the most unusual individual. At the same time, there are some that have been around for a long time and have stood the test of time. Those that have proven themselves in the lives of other people and for which there is a great deal of available evidence for ready examination are worthwhile looking at and considering for adoption.

However, before you rush willy-nilly into accepting something to believe in, it is worthwhile seeing whether it meets some basic criteria, for if it doesn't, it may let you down when you need shoving up the most.

Any philosophy of life must take into account the nature of man, and the fact that man is always at war with other men and with himself, since man is basically self-centered. The eight criteria I suggest for your consideration are

1. *It must be based on some knowledge:* It is not possible to intellectualize faith in anything, *but* neither can you believe in something about which you know nothing or in which your knowledge base is false. This is why there is so much trouble today in many of the organized religions. The older generation built a fairy tale, today's middle-agers grew up believing that fairy tale, and their children have grown up with next to nothing. Even knowing so little, the hypocrisy of their parents is obvious, and the conflict is easy to understand. Thus we have the middle-ager in the pew facing problems that his "cotton-candy" faith can't help him with. (Why cotton candy? It melts under very little pressure and heat.) And their children have drugs, alcohol, and sex. Too strong an indictment? The facts say otherwise.

2. *A personal philosophy must be reasonable:* If your philosophy is to be yours and it is to work, it must be all yours. You must know what it is, and you must be able to live with it. To begin with, a person who says, "I am a pragmatist" and doesn't know what a pragmatist is or who believes in an incorrect definition, simply is not a pragmatist. Moreover, once you know what you want and are and believe in, you must have the ability of achieving whatever goals are related to it.

3. *A personal philosophy must be comprehensive:* A personal philosophy must provide you with the ability to meet "all" life's normal crises, with balance. At the death of a close loved one, you should be saddened—at the loss of a job, you should be sad and deeply disappointed—at the true realization that you have lived half or two-thirds of your life, it is normal to feel regret—but in none of these should you be paralyzed (mentally) and thus incapable of appropriate, effective action. Your personal philosophy must enable you to maintain perspective in all these and in many other conditions as well.

4. *Your personal philosophy must be consistent:* Your personal philosophy must be independent of time and retain its

integrity in all its facets for all applications of it. As human beings we frequently make demands on fate or whatever it is that we hold accountable for the direction of the universe. When tragedy strikes, we often ask with great emotion, "Why me?". Isn't it strange that when something has gone particularly well, however, we almost never say (with or without emotion), "Why me?".

5. *Your personal philosophy must require full commitment:* A personal philosophy that can be put on or taken off like a coat, or which envelops less than the whole person, is nothing at all.

6. *Your personal philosophy must be always at hand:* Although the statement may be considered overly simplistic, a personal philosophy is a set of beliefs and a belief is a part of the believer. That is to say, it is part of the guiding force that directs the person's behavior, cannot be put aside or shut off, and cannot operate part time. It is possible for a person to deliberately act against his own beliefs, but the motive must be strong and the need for such action great.

In this matter, a person may frequently fail to act on his beliefs, simply because human nature is imperfect and the cliche, "The spirit is willing but the flesh is weak," is, in fact, a truism. With human frailty preventing full adherence to one's beliefs, then, it is indeed difficult to determine whether a stated belief is, in fact, that or merely lip service to an idea. On the other hand, a belief will occupy a greater portion of a person's life than will mere "lip service" and will influence more and different things than will a philosophy that is pretended.

Another way of describing the same thing is to say that a belief cannot be totally ignored except when it is convenient or fulfills a special need. For example, one of the problems of too many religious people is that they attempt to compartmentalize God. That is to say, God is a part of their lives between 11:00 A.M. and noon on Sundays, and for approximately two minutes at bedtime every night. In both cases, the liturgy is mechanical and the equivalent of, "Now I lay me down to sleep." The effect of such belief and practice is obvious. And, the reason so many "Christians" are leaving the church today is that they never were Christians in the first place—if you follow the idea that a Christian should know what a Christian is and believes in.

In brief, a belief can be held and imperfectly acted on, but not pretended.

7. *Your personal philosophy must make you know that you are worthwhile:* The person who sees himself as being of little value has no real reason to exist and certainly will not have motivation to grow, develop, and make effective use of his abilities.

If you are to strive for happiness and be happy, your personal philosophy must be built on hope and must be firmly set in the concept that you are a meaningful part of the human race with a positive contribution to make to it.

8. *Your personal philosophy must permit you to reach your potential:* Many of the beliefs held by people today are founded in the concept that it is sufficient to do what you want to do, for, "Whatever feels right must be right." I will run the risk of being accused of being an advocate of the Protestant work ethic and say that man cannot achieve his full potential or very much else that is worthwhile without self-discipline and the obligation to work. Your philosophy should encompass self-discipline and work as positive virtues, without apology and, although in proper balance, without reservation.

Step #6: Get and act on the results of a comprehensive physical examination.

Even though a great deal of research on the Mid-Life Crisis is needed, one fact is well established; people who enjoy good health live happier lives than those who don't, and by and large they live longer. Physical examinations are avoided by so many people that many companies, for example, have had to make them mandatory for their executives.

More than ever before, there is good reason today for an annual physical examination. To be repetitious of much advertising, our medical technology now is such that many problems can be solved before they become serious. Even many cancers can be treated if detected early enough. But it is difficult to convince people of this fact. In men, one out of five are found to have some sort of treatable prostate probelms—treatable if detected early enough.

Go to your doctor: find out what you need to do to achieve and stay in good health—and do it!

Another facet of this same recommendation is that you should learn to live *with* your body. On the surface, that statement may seem rather simple minded, but not nearly so much so as what most people do. For example, take a look at what you do to your body and then take a look at what you do to your automobile. If your automobile engine begins to act up, you will take it to a skilled mechanic for diagnosis and repairs. If your body begins to act up, chances are very good you (with no medical training) will prescribe aspirin (without a diagnosis), ignore it out of fear of finding out what the facts are, go to an equally ignorant friend for a diagnosis, or try to find out if someone has read an article on such symptoms in any popular magazine lately. Believe it or not, none of the foregoing is said in the least bit facetiously.

In another sense, listening to your body can also tell you a great deal that, if followed, can be beneficial. For example, some middle-agers find that they grow sleepy in the middle of the afternoon. Most employers would be horror stricken (erroneously) to think of an employee taking an hour's nap between 2:00 and 3:00 P.M., yet some executives I know are doing exactly that. The rationale they follow is that because they work enough hours as it is, an hour's nap will not be missed, but far more importantly, going back to work refreshed makes the last several hours far more productive than would be the case otherwise.

Another common complaint of middle-agers is occasional difficulty of sleeping at night. The remedies typically fall into two categories. First, some take over-the-counter sleeping pills. Second, the remainder toss and turn and usually wake up exhausted in the morning. Some time ago I found that when this happened to me, I, instead of trying to fight sleep (since I also don't believe in taking any type of drugs unless as a true last resort) would turn on the light and read until I got sleepy, get up and watch television, work, or go for a walk. This kind of an approach usually permits me to go back to sleep in short order and wake up refreshed.

Finally, a great deal has been written in recent years about the problem of stress. Many systems have been devised and advice has been given on how to avoid stress or of how to deal with it. If such a system works for you, then I would say use it. If you have not found a satisfactory means of dealing with stress, then I would suggest that you take an honest look at yourself, attempt to find out what is wrong, and, failing that, go see your physician.

A checklist you might follow, for example, would look like this:

Stress Checklist

1. Conduct a self-appraisal (see Step #4 again).

   a. What is it that "sends you up the wall"? Is it your personality: are you impatient, perfectionist, overly demanding, indecisive, or what?

   b. Are there situations over which you have no control that bother you?

   c. Or is it something else?

2. If you can identify the problem area, the answer should automatically suggest itself. For example,

   a. If it is a personality problem such as impatience or perfectionism, be aware of these facts and work to control them. Find out whatever means is necessary to cause that to happen.

b. If you are indecisive, plan to set conditions so that indecision will not be a problem. Some of the things you might do is make a schedule, set priorities, establish ground rules for decision making, and involve other people—or whatever may help.

c. If you can't control your job, consider changing it. If you cannot change your job, try the suggestions that follow.

3. Relax (at least once a day).

a. Sit and force tension-producing things out of your mind. *You* must find the key to do this. It can be done.

b. Total distraction. Even the idiot box (television) can serve a useful function in this regard. Force it into a constructive role in your life.

c. Violent exercise—as much as you can take—but *SEE YOUR DOCTOR FIRST*. Get his advice and follow it!

d. If necessary, obtain professional help. You might try a psychologist, psychiatrist, clergyman, or see #9 and #10 below.

Step #7: Set up a flexible game plan
for the rest of your life.

At this point, if you have done Steps #1 to 6 properly you are ready to begin putting together a plan whereby you can get the most out of the rest of your life.

There is no question that what I have suggested thus far, and will suggest from this point on, requires some work. It is a cliche—nevertheless true—that nothing worthwhile in life is easy. The real secret to success in anything, especially in planning your life, is *commitment*. The payoff will be in direct proportion to the effort you are willing to make and the degree of self-discipline you can exercise in sticking to what you have begun. A halfhearted job can produce few real results.

Commitment will produce results, not on a one-to-one basis—life is too unpredictable for that—but certainly on a far greater than chance basis. Thus if you are not convinced by this time that the potential result is worth the effort, then you would be better off stopping here, for you are sure to be disappointed.

Even with good commitment, there are two additional cardinal rules that are vital to any human endeavor.

1. Planning. Anything works better if it is planned, "Playing it by ear" is necessary for far too much of our lives. Sometimes we are lucky, but more often, the results show that some forethought could have helped us accomplish the task quicker, better, or more efficiently. Even a little forethought is valuable, because there are usually several ways of doing the same thing and almost always one is better than the others. This is particularly true when planning something as complicated as your own life, because the decisions involved will have to take into account a myriad of elements, many of which have unknown components and many others of which are in a constant state of change. Planning will give you at least a fighting chance to take into account as many as possible of all the things that are going to be important throughout the rest of your life.

2. Writing it Down. Anything that is planned will improve in completeness and clarity if written down. Frequently, I ask people about their personal plans and goals, and senior executives about the goals and plans of the organizations they head. Usually I receive answers suggesting the existence of plans and goals, and often am presented with examples. However, when I push on to get a complete list, specifically, when I go after "action plans," I usually end up with next to nothing.

People who "have things in their minds" usually have vague ideas that are incomplete and full of holes. Those inadequacies always come to light when the ideas are committed to writing but are easily glossed over or are invisible when tucked away in a person's mind, where the gaps and inconsistencies are not exposed to the light of day. This matter of writing things down is acknowledged to be a pain in the neck. However, it is so important that it cannot be stressed enough. Indeed, because it forces you to think, people have developed many ways of defending themselves for not doing it. For example, a typical "cop-out" is, "I know what I want to say, but I just can't put it into words." This is sheer nonsense. If it can't be written down, it can't be followed as a prescription or roadmap to achievement of an objective. To accomplish a goal, someone has to "do" something. Behavior can be described. In the case of a life plan, a written document is essential.

The planning process involves three stages: preparation, goals, and action plans.

A. Preparation

Getting ready to put together a plan is very simple and consists of two aspects. One of these is physical and the other is mental.

1. Physical Aspect. Gather together all the information you have generated through Steps #1 to 6. All the information should be in usable form, stated as simply as possible, and prepared for mechanical manipulation appropriate to your personal likes and dislikes. For example, some people will put one idea each on 3" × 5" cards, using different colors of cards for likes and dislikes, personality characteristics, practical considerations, and the like. Other people simply use the lists themselves; others follow other systems. Your approach should be designed to best meet your personal needs.

2. Mental Aspect. Earlier in this section I spoke of the matter of commitment, and I believe fully that it is a vital requirement to doing the planning job effectively. Beyond that point, though, why not try to "psych yourself up" in terms of what you are doing. What you are launching into should be one of the greatest adventures of your life and something for which you are better prepared than you ever have been in your life to date. It is an ideal time to take an active role in controlling your own destiny rather than merely "letting life happen to you" as is true of most people. It should give you a sense of power, and it should be positive! There are many jokes about middle age and even more about old age. One I heard a long time ago goes something like this, "Getting old means that practically everything is something you have to live with or live without." That is *negative* thinking. Life is *change!* Change is always *from* something, but it is also always *to* something. You can do absolutely nothing about what it is from, but you can do a great deal about what your life is going to be.

B. Goals

Having taken a long look at yourself and having done a thorough self-analysis, you should have a good picture of your own needs, abilities, characteristics, potentials, likes and dislikes, and the realistic restrictions on what you can do. The process of self-analysis alone, much less an evaluation of the data themselves, should give you a new perspective on your own life that will suggest targets for you to aim at and illuminate a wealth of ideas that need to be investigated. On the basis of all those data, you should set up three sets of goals:

1. *Long-term:* The entire remainder of your life—assume normal retirement age plus 20 years.
2. *Mid-term:* From today until you retire from your normal working career.
3. *Short-term:* The next 1 to 5 years.

The process of goal setting is not easy, nor is it something you will do well the first time through. You will find that long-term goals tend to be rather general (they should be) and that short-range goals will probably be too ambitious.

Only with time and experimentation can you hit the proper balance between generality and specificity and what is both realistic and possible on the one hand versus too much to accomplish on the other.

For example, typical long-term goals include such things as:

• Happiness
• A home in some retirement area (Florida, Arizona, California, or your birthplace).

Typical short-range goals include such things as:

• Put my marriage back in order.
• Get out of this miserable rat race and open my own business. (See pp. 29 to 31 for a discussion of irrational job changes.)

Long-range goals are necessary as an overall guide. If they are sufficiently realistic and carefully enough thought through, then mid-term and short-range goals can take on added significance, but they must be consistent with them.

Short-range goals that require an overhaul of interpersonal relationships can be (although a major job) realistic if supplemented by proper attitudes and effort. Others, such as opening one's own business, may be overly ambitious, depending on what that business will be and all of the preparation necessary to bringing it into existence. (Many small businesses are begun every year and fail because the owner was long on faith and short on both planning and capital.)

On the other hand, goals that are totally achievable and do not require you to "reach out" are probably unworthy of your potentials and capabilities. A fine balance is needed here, which is why I described the goal-setting process as one you must learn by effort and by trial and error.

There is another way of looking at the process I am describing here as goal setting. This concept, which was introduced to the business world some time ago, has a great deal of face validity and is "assumed" by a great many executives, while in fact, it isn't really done at all in very many places.

To review the concept in a much oversimplified form, there are three essential parts to the process:

1. Set a goal.
2. Develop a plan for achieving the goal.
3. Establish a means of measuring the extent to which the goal is achieved in some predetermined time limit.

Again, in a very oversimplified and modified fashion, goal setting goes on in the early part of most people's lives. (Indeed, on second thought, *everyone* does some goal setting, at least in the early years of their lives.) For our purposes here, I would suggest four major time periods as pertinent to our overall subject (mid-life) and the specific process of setting up a flexible game plan for your life. These are

Stage #1: Youth. All young people set goals, beginning with the very earliest of years. As rudimentary as such may seem they include statements like:

• I want to be a doctor when I grow up.
• I want to get married when I grow up and have six children.
• When I get bigger I want to be a policeman.
• Can I be an astronaut when I grow up?
• I want to go to college after high school.

All these are goals in a very real sense, and the behaviors attendant to those aspirations can be thought of as the planning I mentioned earlier. As for measuring devices, at that stage in life, it's usually all or nothing. Nevertheless, the basic concepts of goal setting are fulfilled.

Stage #2: Young Adult. In the young adult years some of the earlier goals have been abandoned, some have been realized, some new goals have been set, and some old goals are now being refined. The goal setting done at this stage is far more sophisticated than that carried out earlier. The primary difference here is that the young adult has a great deal more information to work with than he did as a child, and with maturity has come an awareness of the restrictions that surround all human endeavors.

Stage #3: Mid-Life. At this juncture, unrealized goals assume more emphasis than they should, in most cases, primarily because instead of being treated with proper perspective, the unrealized goal is seen as a lost opportunity that can never be achieved.

In a real sense, this point summarizes a great deal of what I have said elsewhere in this book. In brief, life should be a never-ending process of goal setting. Goals need to be set as guidelines—guidelines to the self-discipline man needs if he is to function effectively in society and if he is to achieve any substantive part of what his abilities have made possible.

Every day a person lives he gains more data about himself, his life, the world in which he lives, and his opportunities. With these data, the goals he sets can and should be revised. Such revision should take into account not only basic information, but also your awareness of your values as they shift, your doubts as they grow, and your sources of satisfaction as they change.

In a very real sense, my statements here make me sound like the ultimate pragmatist who reduces everything to the practical level of mechanism. I will admit that I am a pragmatist, but within the definition of that classification, I recognize and include much that many people might not consider to be "practical." For example, I believe that it is important for everyone to dream and to have a dream. Ideals are an essential part of living, for they enlarge your vision and help to stretch your ambitions and abilities. My only concern and caution is that a proper balance between dreaming and practical reality be maintained—that balance you must determine in your own life, for it is fully dependent upon your own assessment of your responsibilities, desires, goals and potentials.

Few people have ever regarded me as a romantic, and I recognize that there may be something missing in the grammar, but despite everything else, I believe that as long as life lasts, the stars will be there to be reached out for, and this leads to Stage #4.

Stage #4: Beyond Mid-Life. The process described above should go on as long as a person lives. It may well be that reality will suggest that as a person gains more and more years, his goals must be more short range in terms of intended accomplishment, but there should be goals.

There is a future for everyone. Viewed realistically, very few people at age 45 can "guarantee" that they will live any more days or weeks than can a person who is 85.

Reduced to its simplest terms, life is a lot more fun and a great deal more satisfying if you are attempting to achieve a specific thing and in fact reach that goal than it is if you flop along from day to day without point or purpose to your existence other than simply that—existence.

C. Action Plans

Once your goals are set, the next step in the process is to supplement these with action plans that will bring them into reality. With only a few exceptions, I have made a deliberate attempt in this book to avoid using examples and case studies. The reason for this is that people tend to follow examples, but you and your life are unique. What has worked for someone else quite probably will be totally inappropriate for you. What you need to do is "your own thing" and to do this with guidance, which is why Steps #7 and #9 are so important.

Suffice it to say, your plans should be highly specific and in as close accord as possible to all of the information you gathered in Steps #1 through #6. At this point, it does not matter whether the action plan is geared to the achievement of a long-term or a short-range goal, for it can be specific in either case. To buy a retirement home may require a special savings plan *now* that demands you open a savings account and allocate a certain amount of money to go into that each week or month. Some specific action plans can be very simple—others will be quite complex. For example:

1. On the Vocational Level. What do you plan to do with the rest of your career? Various possibilities include:

a. Stay where you are until retirement and then go into a retirement that has been planned and prepared for.

b. Stay in your current position but begin (on your own time) to develop a skill or business that will gradually, over time, become full time and replace your present job.

c. Stay in your present job and begin preparing for a job change at the right moment into the right job (possibly within the organization for which you currently work).

Throughout this book I have spoken about people who make job changes in response to the emotional pressure of a Mid-Life Crisis, and I have even suggested that a well-thought-out job change can be highly desirable. One point, however, has not yet come up, and this has to do with the nature of the organization in which you take that new job. The assumption is that when a job change is made, it will be to another organization, but this need not necessarily be the case. If you are fortunate enough to be employed by an organization that has the welfare of its employees at heart, it may well be that a job change within the organization would be the best alternative. I recognize that there are some organizations where your job will be in jeopardy if you dare to mention that your present job is not fully satisfying, but you must make that determination before you set your plans. Assuming that you are not working for a "klutz," it is very likely that the organization can be of great assistance in identifying jobs for which you may have transferable skills or unrealized potential. Even further, the company could help by pointing out training you might take and even show a willingness to assist you in that endeavor.

Finally, staying in the same organization where you currently work makes sense from another standpoint. You have already gained seniority and invested a good bit of time there. If you can achieve your goal of finding a job that will give you greater satisfaction and permit you to be more productive while retaining all that you have gained where you are, why not take advantage of what you have available?

d. Move to a new job right now.

2. On the Personal Level

a. Stop wasting your time in meaningless extracurricula activities by resigning from those organizations in which you are doing nothing and which thus serve no purpose.

b. Begin "trying out" new activities in which you can do something worthwhile—both for yourself and for someone else.

c. Develop a hobby—one that can benefit you either mentally or physically, or both.

d. Plan to keep active mentally. This may sound like a strange suggestion, but not really, when you consider the evidence we have to date. First, far too many people put their brains into neutral right after retirement. Second, the slender evidence we have available today points rather strongly to the fact that people who keep active mentally can continue growing and even stave off senility—or at least slow the aging process considerably.

What do I mean by keep active mentally? I do not mean mental activity such as that involved in adding up bridge points or a golf score. What I do mean is doing something that requires that you *think*. Here again, you have to pick what the thing will be, because if it isn't interesting, you won't do it, and if it doesn't provide satisfaction, you won't keep it up. However, within that frame of reference, why not write a book (it doesn't matter if it is ever published, but you might surprise yourself); invent something (so what if it doesn't work, try something else); lay out a realistic, practical plan for feeding all of the hungry people in the world, taking into account all of the political as well as economic problems involved (send it to your congressman); design and build an organization to accomplish some specific objective, such as helping to control dog leash-law violations in your local area; and so on and so on and so on.

Thomas Jefferson made the point that people who work for the government should do so for only short periods. I believe that his idea was to urge those who are best qualified to take time out of their careers to give their talents to their country. Why can't you do the same thing? Run for the local school board, or volunteer to take on some special activity with that group.

The list of things one can do to keep mentally active is endless. So too are the cheap imitations that seduce people into thinking that they are being mentally active when, in fact, they have already gone to sleep.

3. On an Emotional Level

a. Go back and mend some fences where you have let interpersonal relationships deteriorate, over which you are carrying a load of guilt feelings.

In mending those fences, take a long look at what happened in the first place and see if there isn't some sort of a lesson that you can learn from what occurred. Everyone, even hermits, must interact with other people. Frequently, those meetings are neither positive nor satisfying, and equally often, in such situations you conclude (with a great deal of justification) that the other person has been the cause of the problem because he has been emotional rather than logical, pig-headed rather than open-minded, and sometimes just plain downright rotten.

A question you seldom if ever ask yourself, however, is "Is that person just the way he appears to be, or is he reacting to the same characteristics (or some similarly prompting stimulus) in my behavior or personality?''. You see, they are themselves (which is complicated enough all by itself), but what you see is also frequently a mirror, to some extent, of your behavior and the impact that your behavior has on them.

These facts have led to many cliches and philosophical sayings, most of which are based on fact, such sayings as:

- Laugh and the world laughs with you.
- It's hard to be angry at someone who keeps smiling.
- Gee, but it's so nice to be around him, you can't feel downhearted in his presence.

These, and many more, reflect the same idea. Our interpersonal relationships are built on action *and* reaction. It's important to be able to recognize which is which and to be able to control your own behavior to produce the kind of response you want in others.

b. Begin to learn to live for "now and tomorrow."

c. Set up specific actions calculated to improve the quality of your marriage.

What you are *willing* to do is a good measure of how important it is to you. Your values are expressed in your behavior, not in your wishes and desires.

Step #8: Set up a follow-up program.

The process described in Steps #1 to 7 is never ending. It must go on throughout the rest of your life.

In the title of Step #7, it was stated that you should set up a "flexible" game plan, and that is exactly what it must be. In the strictest definitions of the *words,* life is change. And, because your life is an endless succession of changes, your plans must also be modifiable and modified as each new event occurs.

By and large, major changes will be relatively infrequent, yet as you grow and develop, your circumstances shift, your skills are magnified, and your physiological life progresses, your plans (and possibly even your goals) must keep pace.

To accomplish and take change into account, it is not necessary to establish an elaborate program or do anything unusual. If you have done your homework well in Steps #1 through #7 and commit yourself to a constant update as changes occur, the follow-up program should be automatic. At the same time, it is highly desirable to establish frequent checkpoints (once a year or every six months) to review the entire program, measure the progress you have made, and "tune up" your goals and plans.

If this follow-up step is taken, it will involve very little work. If it is not taken, the entire program can go down the drain.

Periodic checks can reveal progress that has been made, highlight achievements, reveal weaknesses, and bring oversights to light. It is essential!

The process described here is very much akin to what in the business world is called management by objectives. Step #8 (here) is nothing more or less than the annual evaluation of progress and redefinition of goals for the next period of time.

Take a look at what I am suggesting in terms of what you actually have to do. Given a set of written goals and action plans, and having provided for some means of recording progress during the year, the evaluation session can be a great deal of fun. In fact, if you are able to do all of this with your wife, you might even go away for a weekend and combine a two- or three-day vacation with the evaluation/follow-up process. (As an aside, this point is worthy of elaboration. Most of what I am suggesting throughout this book can be fun if approached properly. For example, I have suggested and talked about the steps thus far as they relate to you as an individual. There is no reason in the world why your wife can't do the same thing at the same time, and there is every reason why she should. You are sharing your lives in everything else. The process suggested here is aimed at the very heart of your life individually and your two lives mutually.)

Step #9: Get help—whether you need it or not, because you do!

Most Mid-Life Crisis problems can be solved by the individual, himself, once he recognizes the problem for what it is, digs into the facts and thus has reassurance that he can deal with the problem on his own. It is surprising how many people to whom I have given guidance in this area have expressed a concern over whether or not they will need to see a psychiatrist. With reassurance that this will probably not be necessary (and even if it is, it wouldn't hurt) there is a visible reduction in tension. With further reassurance that following the plan we have established will solve the overall problem, they are usually in a position to do so.

There are three major barriers to solving Mid-Life Crisis problems, AND, interestingly enough, to preventing or avoiding them in the first place. These are

1. *Lack of Time for Self-Examination:* In the very busy lives we lead, it is rare that we take time to look at ourselves, be sensitive to warning signs, examine our needs, or seriously plan for our personal futures. Each one of us has a great deal of time that *could* be devoted to such reflection. The problem is to exercise the self-discipline necessary, to turn off the television set, to resign from that organization in which you are really accomplishing nothing anyway, to admit that your weekly bridge session with the Smiths is more habit than enjoyment or that reading the Sunday newspaper from cover to cover is not done for enjoyment or personal edification

but rather so that you will be ready to participate in an "intellectual" conversation should it arise, even though it rarely does. (Too many executives spend too much time learning or doing things to impress other people such as their boss, under the mistaken impression that this will advance their careers. Much of this is waste time. But, to pick up that "waste" time you might have to develop the courage to admit to your boss that you *had* anticipated going through life without becoming well-informed on the mating habits of the Australian kiwi bird.)

When you are ready to stop kidding yourself, you will find that no matter how "busy" you are, you really can find a great deal of time that can be invested in making your own life happier, more productive, and better prepared to meet or avoid problems.

2. *Lack of Objectivity:* Again, being redundant, there is no way you can be as objective about yourself, with yourself, as you really should be in planning your own life. When the human animal was designed originally, it was constructed with a great many built-in protective devices, psychological as well as physical. Those psychological protective devices are called defense mechanisms, and they serve many very useful functions. In addition, however, they also help you to avoid work and reality by helping you to gloss over the true significance of a shortcoming (making it seem harmless and acceptable in your own mind), avoid thinking about things that are unpleasant and mix fancy with fact when considering your strengths and potentials.

A beautiful example of a defense mechanism is operating right now for many of the people reading this series of paragraphs. Some of you are now saying, "Maybe he's right about others, but I sure know myself and I don't do those things." The concept that we judge others by their behavior and ourselves by our intentions was never more true!

3. *Most People Don't Have a True Confidant:* The only realistic solution to not being able to be totally candid with yourself is to have someone else whom you can talk to *openly, freely without reservation, and about even those thoughts that you find difficult to accept as your own, even though they are.*

Call it ego, pride, or whatever. We can't admit (especially men and most particularly those in positions of authority such as executives and professionals) that we are afraid of something, have a weakness or doubts about ourselves. Instead, we blind ourselves to the facts of reality, even though they may be obvious to everyone else and/or worry and stew about a problem until it gets out of hand and begins to affect our peace of mind and the lives of those whom we influence. In the first instance, you shut it out—deny it exists —and so it just lays there waiting to trip you up at an appropriate time. (The appropriate time is *always* the wrong time.) In the latter instance, most of the things you worry about, brought out into the light of day and looked at objectively, are not worth worrying about, but cannot be seen that objectively by yourself.

Everyone needs someone to talk to—someone who will listen and, who, in most cases, need not even respond. This is especially true for executives who build up internal anxiety under the pressure of stress and need someone to talk to, simply as a safety valve.

The many effects of stress, tension, pressure, and anxiety are well known. Outstanding among these are distortions in perception (particularly about the self), confusion of inferences with facts, and blocking on things that are unpleasant—to mention but a few.

Thus to meet an existing crisis or plan for the future, you need someone who can help you gain perspective and objectivity, someone who can point out fallacies in your thinking, raise questions about your ability to accomplish goals, and see both your strengths and abilities in their true light when you take them for granted or underrate them—and do all of this without turning you off from:

- Your project (plan).
- Yourself.
- Him (or her).

Admittedly, this is a tall order!

Where and How Do You Find a Confidant? Finding someone whom you can talk to, as I have described it, can be very easy or very difficult, depending on your personality makeup, particular personal circumstances, financial resources, how serious you are about the project, and, to some extent, luck.

I will start off by saying it is not easy to accomplish this in the most entirely satisfactory manner, but it can be done. You have three *general* options:

1. The Quick and Easy Method—Go to a Professional. Any competent psychologist, psychiatrist, or vocational counselor can be of great help and probably will be in the shortest space of time. These professionals know what they are doing and will not waste time. But, they charge fees, some of which are quite high.

I strongly advocate that these professionals be seen when you have a personal problem that is causing you unhappiness, just as you would call an appropriately competent specialist to set a broken leg, treat a case of acne, or diagnose and treat a headache and fever.

Many of the people I see who have Mid-Life Crisis problems need only one or two appointments. In those meetings, much of the advice I give is contained in this book (personalized to their individual needs), supplemented by follow-up to discuss and approve a newly formulated long-range plan. Sometimes I administer aptitude or interest tests, but usually we just talk.

HOWEVER
THE MAIN POINT OF THE BOOK

A vast majority of Mid-Life Crisis problems can be dealt with readily and easily by the individual, without professional help and in relatively short order. The 10 steps set forth in this chapter are a suggested means of doing exactly that.

Professional help can be very useful and should be used far more than it is. (Some day people will get over the stupid ideas they have about psychologists and psychiatrists—admittedly, the behavior of some of the professionals doesn't help in that regard—and when they do the true value of the professions will begin to be appreciated.) But for the kinds of problems and life planning we are talking about here, I do not believe that such professional help is necessary *for most people*.

2. Generally Available Help—Not Quite So Quick and Easy. There are many people from whom you can get *some* advice and help, in a total process of life and mid-career planning. In each case, however, there are cautions, conditions, and limitations you should be aware of.

There are many professionals with whom you can talk concerning specific questions and about some topics, for example, your physician, attorney, personnel specialist at work, and others, especially if you know what you want to find out and are able to evaluate what you learn in the light of everything else you know about yourself.

Other professionals are a mixed bag and must be sorted out carefully. Your clergyman, for example, can be a great deal of help *if* he has some training and experience and is himself able to be objective. A well-meaning pastor, who looks only for good in every situation and is overly concerned with comfort and kindness, may help you to "feel good." However, this is not the objective of the relationship I am talking about here.

3. The Best Way. The best way of all is to find a confidant— a friend—with whom you can be completely open and frank, one who is able to be objective, honest, enduring of your idiosyncracies, and truly helpful.

The problem with this solution is that you cannot—most people cannot—set out deliberately to find a confidant, for friendship is involved, and it cannot be programmed or forced.

Accordingly, the search for a confidant might take years—
AND I CANNOT STRESS THIS TOO STRONGLY—picking the
wrong person will probably cost you a friend and cause you a
great deal of embarrassment. (Any pre-middle-age person who
is interested in avoiding the Mid-Life Crisis can do himself a
major favor by looking to this one area alone at an early stage
in his life.) To repeat, such a relationship—friendship—cannot
be forced. However, it *can* be helped along—usually by an honest expression of your own emotions and feelings of friendship,
as such is natural to do.

As you read this suggestion, I hope you recognize the true
significance of what I am suggesting. I am telling you that you
should actively seek out and consciously foster a relationship
that under most circumstances develops best unaided.

Only because the end result is so important am I suggesting that you consciously become involved in something that
usually takes place without your conscious knowledge *and*
works best that way.

The process (schematically) goes something like this:

- You find someone whom you like.
- You ask yourself, "Hey, I wonder if this person could be-
come a close friend?".
- You set about fostering the relationship.

What I am really suggesting is that you merely be *conscious*
of the fact that in your lifetime you have a *need* for close
friends, because man is a gregarious animal who cannot function as effectively alone as he can with other people. Also,
few people give very much thought to the selection of their
friends. Man is by nature a gregarious creature who has a need
to share himself emotionally with others. Indeed, he becomes
whole as he is part of a group—as he shares himself with others
—especially one other person.

Today, far too many people find themselves in middle age
with a lot of acquaintances and no really close friends. (Loneli-

ness is still one of the major dangers of middle as well as old age.)

In brief, I am suggesting that you take a look at your friends and try to deepen the relationships you have with one or two of them. How you do that depends entirely on your own personal makeup and that of your friend. If you are clumsy or make your friend uncomfortable, you are probably going to weaken the relationship. Also:

• The wrong one is worse than none at all.
• Circumstances such as a job transfer may bring about a physical separation that can create a problem.
• A close personal relationship can lead to a dependent relationship. (You don't want someone who is going to make your decisions for you. Rather, you need someone who can help you keep your own thinking straight.)

For purposes of clarification, there is still another way you can look at the task I am suggesting here. What I am suggesting is not an active process whereby you go around tapping people on the shoulder and saying to them, "Hey, I want you to be my friend!". Rather, the process is more one of clarifying attitudes (your own) such as:

• Recognizing the need for friends—in this case a particular friend.
• Recognizing that friendship is a two-way street that doesn't "just happen," but is the result of shared experiences, mutual interests, and emotional involvement.
• Recognizing that in any interpersonal relationship each person has to "give" more than he "receives." A good example of this is found in the Bible in Chapter 13 of First Corinthians. (Don't be frightened off by the Biblical reference. Non-Christians are permitted to read the Bible just like anyone else without committing themselves to anything. Even the most hard-nosed businessman—even should he be an atheist—would profit from reading Exodus, Chapter 18, Verses 13–26.)

In the kind of relationship I am talking about, your confidant:

• Must be someone with whom you can speak openly and without reservation, about what may well be very personal matters, even on such topics as your sex life, your personal finances, and your religious beliefs.

• Must be someone with whom you can reveal your thoughts and beliefs as listed above, while still maintaining a social relationship with you.

• Must be able to disassociate him or herself from your problems *sufficiently* to be able to deal with your concerns and questions objectively and in a rational manner.

• Should be in a position such that he can disagree with you without being argumentative and still be able to see your defense mechanisms for what they really are.

• Must be readily available when needed, and

• Share your feelings about your relationship sufficiently that your friendship will be able to stand the strain created by your rebellion against facing facts when those facts are unpleasant.

The *ideal confidant* would be your wife. Unfortunately, too few people have the kind of marital relationship that permits complete honesty and frankness, just as too few people have among their "close friends," someone with whom they can relate on a personal or even an emotional level. On the other hand, recognizing the need to have someone to talk to—openly, freely, frankly, and with sincerity—can provide a golden opportunity to make your marriage into what it should be and may once have been. (If you do have that kind of relationship with your mate, you are most fortunate and have no problem to begin with.)

Again, today we are not only living in a youth culture, but we are also living in a society where there is a strong drive for expressions of individuality. Striving for youth and individuality are excellent when kept within reason, but carried to an extreme in a marriage can cause it to become a marriage of two married-single people or prevent the development of a marriage at all, following the ceremony.

Assuming that your marriage is like most (especially if you are an executive) why don't you try talking to your spouse—on the level of feelings—just as an experiment? If it doesn't work out, you can always go back to the same dumb, insipid relationship you've had in the past. On the other hand, if it does work out, it could be one of the most exciting experiences of your life and provide you with a confidant—eventually—who, in the security of a mature love, can provide:

- Proper perspective.
- Honesty and objectivity.
- The desire to overcome the "blinding" effect of a close personal, emotional relationship.

Believe me, it can work, if you *both* work at it!

For the helper: Being a "helper" is a tough job. Anyone who is suffering from the effects of trauma, in this case a Mid-Life Crisis, is overly concerned with himself and will be hard to deal with, even though he could benefit greatly from special attention and care. Your job will not be easy!

In the case of a married couple, especially, it is extremely important for the helper to recognize several facts of life:

1. A Mid-Life Crisis in particular and most forms of trauma in general involve a complex of emotions and only rarely can be understood on the basis of a single or simple feelings.

2. In the case of a male, particularly, pride complicates the situation. Where there is a sexual involvement, he will more often than not deny that a problem exists and strenuously resist the very help that he so desperately needs and wants.

3. The helper can expect to be rebuffed and even at times rejected and personally attacked. Where emotion is involved, one should not expect logic and reason.

Therefore, if you are the helper, hang in there!

- You must be sensitive to the other person's needs.
- You must expect to find that "little things" will be blown out of all proportion.

- You must be prepared to cover the same ground again and again.
- You must try always to see the problem through the other person's eyes, not your own.

On the surface it doesn't make much sense for a person to resist being helped when they need it desperately and even want it, but he will. (One of the things that make people so interesting is their infinite complexity and never-ending variety.)

Thus, hang in there!

It can and it *will* work—if you *both* work at it!

Step #10: Learn to face life head on!

In the "good old days" (whenever they were) life was pretty basic. Birth, life (with all of its joys and problems), and death were real. Even as recently as my own childhood, I can remember vastly different attitudes and practices. This does not mean that the problems were less painful, but since they were a part of life and accepted as such, they were more easily and readily accommodated. People didn't like dying or look forward to it any more then than now. However, it was more an accepted part of life and less feared, on a relative basis, than is true today, primarily because of a stronger belief in salvation (even if that belief was based on inaccurate perceptions), and thus it created fewer problems. The Mid-Life Crisis, if it existed and I am not sure that it did, at least not in the form it holds today, was far less severe. Quite probably, it fell into the same category as the "growing pains" of adolescence, since that, too, was considered normal and generally dealt with as an everyday phase of life like everything else. The idiocy of "teenage" life which we have seen since World War II caused, I believe, by the concept of grouping, was unknown. Becoming an adult was eagerly sought after and not feared to the point of damaging society.

Middle age was also seen as more of a normal transition than it is today. People did not want to become feeble, senile, and dead, but old age was not feared as it is today. The youth culture hadn't happened yet and old people weren't shoved into nursing homes as soon as they became a burden to their children. There was respect—and love—for older people, some of which still exists but which is becoming far less frequent.

Today, we have gone to extreme lengths to separate ourselves from unpleasantness and divorce ourselves from the reality of life.

• Under the excuse that it is "safer," babies are routinely born in hospitals. The fact is it's "more convenient" that way (mostly, more convenient for the doctor), and the father rarely has an opportunity to participate in one of the most important facets of his marriage. It also doesn't take very many brains to recognize why so many fathers dissociate themselves from their role as a parent—a role that would be far more real if they were actively involved in the birth process itself. (A few men are beginning to insist on being present at the birth of their children. Perhaps this will develop into a trend.)

• With the excuse that it is "safer," people are popped into the hospital for all sorts of trivia today. The facts are that this makes it very convenient for the doctors and the family. And today the medical profession is discovering and proclaiming a wonderful new concept, "hospitals that emphasize outpatient treatment," especially since costs have become so exhorbitant that third-party payers have begun to take strenuous measures in objection.

• Under the excuse of "nerves," people are turning in increasing numbers to tranquilizers. The fact is that, in far too many cases, the person simply doesn't have guts enough (internal resources or a personal philosophy) to face up to a problem and overcome it.

• Under the excuse of "nerves," people are turning in increasing numbers to alcohol. The fact is that, in far too many cases, the person simply doesn't have guts enough to face up to a problem and overcome it.

• Under the excuse of "nerves," people are turning in increasing numbers to drugs. The fact is that, in far too many cases, the person simply doesn't have guts enough to face up to a problem and overcome it.

• Under the excuse of "nerves," people are turning in increasing numbers to cigarettes. The fact is that, in far too many cases, the person simply doesn't have guts enough to face up to a problem and overcome it.

• To hide from the reality of death, people are buried from funeral homes. The facts are that people want to avoid thinking about death and so have built up a ritualistic "rain dance" that at best is sickening in most of its aspects and (for those of you who claim membership in some aspect of the Judeo-Christian tradition) has little or no Biblical support.

This list merely gently scratches the surface of the many ways we have devised to escape from the reality of life. Perhaps the most significant of all for the purposes of the subject of this book is marriage. In the past 10 years I have attended about a dozen weddings. The ceremonies are either standard or "unusual," but beginning with the reception, an automatic-robot-like ritual begins that supersedes personal inclination, a natural expression of love, and even (as the divorce statistics show) the development of love. It goes something like this (performed by robots):

Click! Click! Now–is–the–time–for–the–reception!

Click! Click! Now–is–the–time–for–the–photographs!

Click! Click! Now–is–the–time–for–the–best-man's–toast! (It must be champagne—nothing else.)

Click! Click! Now–is–the–time–for–the–groom–to–dance–with–the–bride–while–everyone–looks–cow-eyed–and–smiles!

Click! Click! Now–is–the–time–for–the–bride's–father–to–dance–with–the–bride! (More cow-eyes and indulgent smiles.)

Click! Click! Now–is–the–time–to–bang–on–glasses–so–the–groom–will–kiss–the–bride!

Click! Click! Now–is–the–time–for–the–bride–to–toss–her–bouquet–to–the–bridesmaids!

(In the interest of time and space I have cut out a great many of the "traditions.")

Click! Click! Now–is–the–time–to–have–a–baby!
Click! Click! Now–is–the–time–to–join–the–P.T.A.!
Click! Click! Now–is–the–time–to–get–a–divorce!

Laugh if you will, but while you're laughing, take a look at the divorce statistics, go to a wedding, and take a look at the people around you—possibly in your own family.

What I am going to suggest is not particularly brilliant nor new. It is born, however, out of the problems listed above that some of the experts on the subject (of which I count myself as one) view with alarm in terms of the effects they are having on the very fabric of our nation.

Even a person with limited intelligence can take a look at the many examples in the history of mankind and draw some comparisons with what is happening in the United States (and other countries as well) today and project what the long-term effect will be.

My suggestion? Stop running away from life and hiding its unpleasantness behind the facade of "tradition" and commercial enterprise.

Do your children a favor. Let them see life in all of its facets. Don't shove your responsibilities as a parent off onto other people (the schools and the church) no more than you should shove your responsibilities to yourself off onto other institutions and organizations and individuals. (Before someone jumps down my throat about this advice: when I suggest that you force your children to participate in life, I am not suggesting free license. One of your responsibilities as a parent is to teach your children a moral code. Our failure in that regard is a national disgrace, and as a consequence we are rushing pell mell down the road to self-destruction. If you want to criticize me for crying doom and gloom—feel free. If you want to suggest that I don't know what I am talking about—I welcome debate on the subject.)

The process I am suggesting is very uncomplicated:

1. When a problem comes up:

  • Don't ignore it.
  • Don't run away from it.
  • Don't try to minimize it.
  • Don't "wait to see what develops."

2. Find out what the problem is before you attempt to take action. A very wise friend of mine, an attorney, told me once that one of his biggest problems is that people always want him to answer a question before they ask the question. We treat problems the same way. Before you rush off pell mell to solve a problem, make sure you know what the real problem is. Chances are very good that once you find that fact out, the entire matter will be considerably less difficult than it appears at first glance and probably quite different.

3. Once you know what the problem is, decide on what action would be appropriate.

4. Wait! (Give yourself time and the chance that the entire matter will look different after a few hours' reflection.)

5. Act!

Obviously, this formula will not work in every instance. However, it will handle a majority of problems that occur between people and will go a long way toward overcoming problems related to the process of living.

Two common but diverse problems will illustrate the point.

1. Your schedule is full, you really have more to do than you have time for, and you are beginning to feel some pressure. At that point your boss gives you an emergency job to do that must be finished immediately and, just at that point, one of your most significant responsibilities develops a critical problem.

Your choices of action are many and varied. Probably the best approach would be:

• Find someplace where you can be totally alone and undisturbed for a short time (5 to 10 minutes), during which make a real attempt to divorce yourself totally from the situation. You must find your own way to relax. Some executives have learned how to meditate—others pray—some read—and a few are able to "get away from things" by "chit-chat" conversation with a colleague.

• Next, reduce the problems, alternatives, priorities, and possible solutions to writing. (Many times, simply putting things down on a piece of paper will suggest the proper solutions and sequence of events to follow.)

• Where impossible conflicts exist, enlist the aid of your boss—he helped to create the problem in the first place. The procedure suggested above will probably help at that point.

2. Your doctor has told you that you have got to learn to relax. An initial reaction might be to start looking for means of recreation that would help you reduce tension. With that kind of an approach, though, you may well aggravate the problem rather than solve it, simply because you didn't try to find out what the real problem is in the first place.

It seems to me that in that situation, a first common-sense step would be to examine every facet of life, identify the tension-producing aspects of it, and determine which of those can be eliminated first. Then you would be ready to start looking for other means of relaxation. For example, suppose you have some friends that you see frequently but with whom you must retain some vestiges of formality. For whatever reason, you cannot relax completely when with them (perhaps there is an element of competition in your relationship, perhaps there is an attempt to impress them on your part, or maybe you like them well enough but just "can't go that last step in relaxing to the point of being comfortable.") Under these conditions, perhaps you should consider eliminating that relationship or of finding a way of carrying it that extra step so that you can relax. In this kind of situation, two simple facts cannot be ignored. First, you must find some way to relax. Second, you have just so many hours available for relaxation.

FINAL NOTE

The 10-step process listed in this chapter is simple but not easy. If you are feeling some of the symptoms of the Mid-Life Crisis and want to get rid of them, these 10 steps will help. If you want to enjoy greater happiness in your life, again, these 10 steps will help.

Unfortunately, *you* have to make the 10 steps work. There are no gimmicks, no pills to take, and no instant solutions. But if you are really serious, it is well worth a try!

I am not accustomed to "playing games" nor sugar-coating simple facts. What I have suggested here requires mature behavior, particularly the expression of maturity that is found in self-discipline. Running the risk of being accused of moralizing, you entered this world with the perception that the entire world was an extension of your own body, and only as you began to grow did you begin to differentiate between yourself and other "things." Even then, initially, you felt that all of the "things" you saw belonged to you and were yours to use as you wished. With still further growth and maturity came the recognition that one cannot manipulate and control the world, but (consistent with your age level) it is necessary to exercise self-discipline and place what you should *and must* do above what *you want* to do.

The immature person continues functioning without regard for personal responsibility, the effect of his behavior on others, and the future. When asked to explain such behavior or intended behavior, the usual reply is, "I want to do it."

In the same vein, no matter what your life has been—*there is HOPE!*

• Has your way been that of adultery? You can put your marriage back together again if you really want to.
• Has yours been the way of deceit on the job? You can rebuild your career, if you really try to.
• Have you lost communication with the important, signifi-

cant people in your life? If you have, you can open those channels by making the effort.

• Have you lost track of where you are going, if indeed you ever knew? You can find out where you want to go and what is realistically possible, if you are willing to commit yourself to that search.

There is hope. And all sorts of things are available to try that you haven't tried yet. Fortunately, one of man's innate characteristics is a stubborn insistence on hope, and that is good. In your case, it should serve to your positive advantage.

Try it! What have you got to lose? Nothing!

6 Note to Top Management

It is no real news to any well-informed executive that the demand for qualified executives is long standing and growing. As with everything else, the causes are many, but it is generally accepted that the primary causes are a combination of the birth rate fluctuations of the Great Depression and World War II (and the effects of these on today's pool of available middle management) along with a continuing rise in business complexity. Thus the demand is high for executives, and the supply is limited. Any loss of productivity among the executive ranks is, therefore, doubly significant. Only slowly is the business world beginning to recognize that the Mid-Life Crisis which can be a nightmare for the individual is also a financial and organizational problem for the company.

In this chapter, I concentrate on the executive and focus my remarks on what top management can do to maintain and enhance his productivity. However, in the real world, my comments apply equally to all employees, executives or not.

Indispensable to business, the fully qualified executive is the product of a lengthy evolutionary process. Corporate management devotes considerable time and effort (which translate into money) to the finding and developing of people who can expertly manage.

Our college system provides a substantial, steady supply of young people who today graduate with as much usable technical information that many older executives needed years to acquire. But only management perspicacity and perseverance produces the executives capable of managing these technically competent subordinates. Both subordinates and the companies suffer when executives' mature managerial skills are impaired or destroyed by something like the Mid-Life Crisis.

It is imperative, therefore, that both companies and individuals alike be alert for the warning signals of this problem, which can affect any individual and does impair the activities of far too many people.

The Mid-Life Crisis can usually be foreseen and checked before it influences, seriously, the individual's performance on the job, endangers his career and personal happiness, and harms his organization.

What happens when middle age approaches?

1. Some very few people begin to physically deteriorate and are unable to maintain characteristic productivity levels.

2. The vast majority of all people are very capable of not only continuing a level of productivity that has been characteristic of them but can also improve on it if they are managed properly and given help when it is needed.

This is not a book on management, so we will pass that one by—reluctantly.

The Mid-Life Crisis, however, is making serious inroads into executive productivity, and only very few individual organizations are attempting to do anything about it. Most such attempts that I have seen are feeble because of being handed over to someone for action who knows nothing about the problem and who is not provided with adequate resources (budget) to tackle the situation properly.

One of the major problems in dealing with the impact of the Mid-Life Crisis on executive productivity is to identify that impact. Like bad management, it will show up when a crisis hits, but the real problem is not seen in an easily recognizable loss. Rather, it is to be found in unrealized profits, missed opportunities, subordinates who leave in disgust for better opportunities elsewhere, and less of everything than should be.

A logical question at this point would be directed toward a determination of the symptoms that management can look for, and this raises an interesting question. A careful rereading of Chapters 3 and 4 will reveal many of the symptoms that management should be sensitive to, but is that enough? In fact, most of the symptoms listed in Chapters 3 and 4 are visible because the problem has gone far enough that it has become a problem, and a crisis is in existence or very soon to occur. Accordingly, what does management look for?

It is essential to keep in mind that symptoms of problems, like everything else to do with people, are highly individualized. Any attempt to list what those symptoms might be would be, in fact, endless.

The answer, unfortunately, is easy to describe, but not that easy to bring about, namely, what management must look for is some *change* from what is *typical* or *usual* behavior for the individual. This means that management must know the individual's behavior and behavior patterns well enough to detect a change when it occurs or begins to occur and be in close enough contact with him to see what is going on when it happens. This sounds rather simple, but it is not. Sir Arthur Conan Doyle made the point repeatedly in his Sherlock Holmes stories that people look at other people all the time but never (seldom?) see them. That is very true! What is needed, then, is some mechanism whereby management can, on a systematic basis, look at its executives and see them clearly enough to know when a change is occurring from a baseline of behavior that is also known.

The biggest handicap management faces in this matter is its own insecurity and thus inability to admit that it is not doing its job as it should. The two statements, "I know my people," and "I know what's going on in my organization and how my people feel," are said to me so often that they sound like a ringing in my ears. *And,* in a vast majority of cases, the speaker is wrong. This is not the place for a treatise on supervisor/subordinate communications or relationships, but the actual *facts* are far different from what management believes the facts to be.

It is the rare chief executive officer, president, executive vice president, or indeed any supervisor who receives an unadulterated, unfiltered statement of opinion from a subordinate. The supervisor may have the purest motives and intentions in the world, but the subordinate is most unlikely to forget that the person he is talking to also controls his compensation, his opportunity for promotion, and even his ability to continue with the organization.

Thus symptoms are detectable, but most likely only if management approaches the problem in a systematic fashion. There are a number of things management can do. Those are the subject of the remainder of this chapter.

WHAT CAN THE ORGANIZATION DO?

Again, the answer has to be, "A lot, but nothing spectacular!". What is needed here, as is true in so many cases, is quite simple. All that is lacking is for someone to take action. The tools are all developed and ready to be used.

A large number of tools and techniques have been devised, tested, and proven to be effective. Most of them are seductively and deceptively simple. If installed by a layman, they will probably fail. Even worse, most members of top management, when reaching the decision that a program is needed, will generally ask for the most sophisticated approach possible and will not accept the fact that the organization (especially top management itself) must grow into the technique, that most likely it will require years of effort.

Accordingly, the first step in this process involves the simple act of accepting facts. Those facts are likely to be unpleasant, but unless that step is taken, your chances of success are very limited. What are some of the facts?

• The attitudes expressed above are commonplace and probably almost universal. Man's (top management) confidence in his unlimited knowledge of human behavior is limitless. A common statement is, "I am no psychologist, but . . . ," and the ensuing statements and action belie the words. The heart of the problem is that most people cannot bring themselves to accept the fact that they are anything less than experts on human behavior simply because they are people too.

• At the same time, executives are supposed to understand people, and for one to admit that he doesn't would be for him to say, "I am not qualified for my job." The vicious cycle thus continues with the following results:

a. Most companies haven't bothered to install even the most simple types of programs that would prevent or detect the Mid-Life Crisis, *or*

b. Have programs that are not sufficiently designed or supported to do the job for which they are intended.

The attitudes of management in most companies are clearly visible in the programs they support and the actions they take. Still today, in this modern world, the personnel department receives the least support of almost any in the company (by support I am talking about management commitment not necessarily just dollars), and its programs are the first to be curtailed when costs must be cut.

Now, what can the organization do? Admittedly, what should be done will work best if it is tailor-made for the specific organization. Within that context, though, the process should consist of two steps and provide for at least four programs:

Step #1: Recognize the problem!
Step #2: Establish programs that will forewarn of an impending problem or identify one if it already exists.

What can be done here is limited only by man's imagination. Some of the more readily available and proven techniques include:

A. Performance Appraisal

Whether we are talking about merit rating, performance appraisal, management by objectives, or whatever, most companies have nothing at all in the way of such a program, and most of those that do exist are inadequate either in design or implementation.

A program, to be effective, does not have to be complex. However, everyone involved must know what they are doing, and top management must be committed to making the program work.

An effective performance-appraisal program (of whatever variety) will not happen overnight. The pay-off—and there *will be* a pay-off *if* the program is done properly—will not be seen for (in many cases) as long as 5 years.

The basic purpose of performance appraisal is to provide information to the organization *and* to the individual on his performance, progress, and growth. It is hard to believe but nevertheless true that the same organization that goes to great lengths to measure the performance of a $3.00-an-hour production worker does nothing to determine the effectiveness of an $85,000 a year executive, even though poor performance of the former will be measured in tens of dollars, whereas poor performance of the latter can often be measured in tens of thousands of dollars.

For example, some time ago, a company asked me to design a performance-appraisal program as a means of overcoming some substantial problems the company recognized. After a total review of the situation I designed a very simple system and described to top management the process whereby that system could be developed and made sophisticated as the executives' capability in its use also grew. It was clear to me that anything more complicated—as a beginning—would fail because of its complexity. A group of young Turks who quite openly admitted they did not "want" to have their performance measured (the fact was that they were afraid of the measurement and what it would bring to light) derided the program because of its simplicity and described it to top management as something that "anyone could have gotten out of a book." That conclusion happens to be true, although the ability to determine the correctness of that solution to the problem could not be derived from reading a book. The end result is that the company still has the original problems, and the young Turks are doing exactly as they please, which is not very productive for the company.

Dozens of other examples could be cited. The end result (conclusion), however, would be the same.

Effective performance appraisal will detect both signs of Mid-Life Crisis problems and productivity problems resulting from other conditions.

Performance appraisal will *not work without* top management commitment . . . commitment of:

- Themselves.
- The resources (time and money) at their command.
- Their organization.

B. Counseling Programs

An effective performance-appraisal program will involve counseling. At the same time, it is possible to have a counseling program independent of performance appraisal. Here, special skills are involved, and it will probably be necessary for the company to employ a trained counselor or establish a working relationship with one who is otherwise employed (in private practice or on a college faculty). Whatever approach is taken, a good bit of time will be required before the programs will be effective. Here, as is also true with performance appraisal, a relationship of trust must be built before employees will "level" with a counselor about personal problems. Anything that violates that trust will destroy the entire program.

It is important to recognize that performance appraisal and counseling, although closely related and interactive, serve different functions and have different purposes.

• *Performance Appraisal:* Measures individual executive productivity serves to identify and overcome problems, identifies potential and stimulate its realization, and provides a framework within which the supervisor and subordinate can work together to accomplish the mutual objectives of the company and the individual. The program also permits the comparison of the individuals and groups at any one point and developmentally over time.

   Properly used, performance appraisal should help to identify mid-life problems before they reach the crisis stage.

• *Counseling:* These programs and sessions are highly individualized and confidential, in which the individual receives help with a personal problem, the nature and extent of which the company will probably know nothing. The payoff for the company comes in terms of maintained or increased productivity on the part of the individual as the inhibiting or blocking problem is removed, and that alone is worthwhile.

C. Mid-Life Crisis Seminars

Recognizing that the Mid-Life Crisis is a reality, why not bring it out into the open, explore its causes, and show how it can be solved?

As has been noted elsewhere in this book, a great deal of research is yet necessary on various facets of the Mid-Life Crisis. On the other hand, we know a great deal and can serve an effective purpose by making sure that those who are subject to or likely to experience the crisis know its symptoms, causes, and solutions.

If the company believes it can be useful, the company could sponsor a Mid-Life Crisis seminar to inform its employees of the nature of the problem and what can be done about it.

If such seminars are made voluntary, some employees will attend out of curiosity, some because they are experiencing a problem, and others because of a genuine desire to learn. Some, however, will stay away because of a fallacious conviction of immortality (as held by Invictus) and some out of fear. The fear may be of discovering something they don't believe themselves able to handle or that by showing up they will be identified by management as having a problem, which could lead to dismissal. (Employee trust is fragile and never as strong as is insecurity.)

Mandatory programs require the skillful handling of professionals who recognize all the varied attitudes that employees bring to such a situation. In my opinion, the mandatory approach is the best one. Only professionals should be in charge of such seminars.

At the very least, such seminars should be made mandatory for executives, even if under the guise of acquainting them with knowledge they will need to carry out their jobs more effectively in dealing with the problems of subordinates.

D. Preretirement Programs

With all that is being written today in the area of retirement and about problems people face because they are not prepared to retire, it is hard to imagine an organization not doing something to help its employees prepare for retirement. Yet, this is exactly the case. Most organizations have a preretirement program that begins and ends on the day the person retires and is confined specifically to an explanation of retirement benefits such as the pension and insurance programs.

A few organizations go one step beyond that and provide

pension and insurance information somewhat earlier—usually a matter of weeks or months.

Only a very few organizations have recognized the major adjustment that is required by retirement and have taken the positive step of establishing a program geared to helping the employee move into retirement gracefully.

The connection between the Mid-Life Crisis and a pre-retirement program is found in the fact that both are concerned with the aging process, postretirement activities, and the retention of one's self-sufficiency.

If a preretirement program is properly designed, it will begin functioning somewhere in the time frame when many people experience Mid-Life Crisis problems. Accordingly, the program should be designed to deal with the crisis on a preventative or remedial basis. In an earlier chapter I dealt with the matter of when middle age occurs and spoke to the ever-present question, "When can I expect the Mid-Life Crisis to hit?". To repeat the essence of the concepts I stated, middle age is as much a state of mind as it is a physiological condition, and the Mid-Life Crisis is so highly individualized that it can begin anywhere from the middle 30s to a very advanced age—or never.

Because of these facts, the chances are very good that many people who would be touched by a properly conceived and conducted preretirement program, would benefit from knowledge of the Mid-Life Crisis.

A FINAL NOTE

Everything in this chapter thus far has been geared to the avoidance or resolving of the Mid-Life Crisis because of the very negative effect it has on executive productivity. In one sense that is a good and sufficient reason for taking action.

On the other hand, the actions that top management can

take—as suggested here—are both well-proven techniques of management (with or without a concern for the Mid-Life Crisis) and/or could be provided by management simply as another fringe benefit to the company's employees. Whichever approach is taken, the company should benefit as, too, will the individual.

7 Note to Housewives

(or, For Women Only)

Chapters 1 through 5 are addressed to male executives, although in reality the things that I said apply equally to males and females, executives or not. In other words, the Mid-Life Crisis is a common human condition that applies to people.

The focus of my work during the past 25 years has been with male executives, and it is from that background, I draw my authority. During the past several years I have broadened my area of research and application. And, without very much surprise, I have found that the same principles apply to all people, in all stations and conditions of life.

Yet, this chapter is addressed to one special group— housewives—because that group shares certain common problems and many common needs and still constitutes a vital core of the structure of our society.

The advice offered in this chapter is nothing more or less than a specific expansion of Steps #1 to 10 in Chapter 5 which will become obvious, I believe, as we proceed.

BASIC CONCEPTS

Before launching into a discussion of the special problems and needs of the group I have termed housewives, it is necessary to recognize three basic concepts that pertain to any discussion of human behavior. Although I will admit to being biased on the subject, I also consider myself to be an expert in the study of human behavior. As such, I know of nothing that rivals the complexity of the human organism or the manifestations of that being, expressed in words and deeds.

A good understanding of the three concepts mentioned above is essential if one is to suggest an appreciation for common problems and suggested solutions thereto. The three concepts are

1. *Individual Differences:* It is generally accepted that no two people who have ever lived have been exactly alike. Although we all share all of the same characteristics, we have them in such a wide variety of degrees and combinations that the possibilities are infinite, and the chances of two people being alike, ever, are extremely remote.

Accordingly, you and I may have the same problem—in general—but in the final analysis it will differ between the two of us to some extent, as should the solution also. In other words, although problems and solutions can be thought of in common terms, the best approach will emphasize the specific individual and what best suits his or her needs.

For example, a common task of most housewives is washing dishes. The odds are extremely high that very few women wash their dishes in exactly the same way. They may use the same water temperature, the same type of cleaning agent, and even the same equipment. However, the way they go about it and how they do it will differ broadly from one person to the next. The same principle applies whether the activity involved is related to housework, child rearing, interior decoration, or even marital relations.

2. *The Principle of Exception:* Over the years we have learned many things about human behavior, in the "why" and "how" people do things. From all of the studies that have been done it is possible to draw certain general conclusions. *HOWEVER,* to any general conclusion about people, one must expect there to be exceptions.

In one sense this is a correlary to the concept of individual differences, and it is an important correlary. For example, it is a normal and generally accepted condition that mothers love their children. The concept of individual differences states that the expression of that love will differ broadly from one mother to another, and the principle of exception states that there will be exceptions to the rule. An entire industry (cosmetics) has been built on the concept that women are concerned enough about their personal appearance to want to improve upon nature. That desire is not universal, however, and there are some women who seem to take delight in making themselves as unattractive as possible.

3. *The Concept of Motivation:* Contrary to popular opinion, motivation is a force within an individual that is expressed outwardly at the discretion of the individual and not something that can be injected or manipulated from the outside. A commonly heard question from executives ignorant of this fact is, "How can I motivate my subordinates?". The fact is, he can't!

It is possible for one person to establish conditions that are favorable to motivation, just as it is possible for a person to do the opposite. For example, if you tell your children that they are incapable of doing something, very likely they will believe it and not try—individually, there will be exceptions to this. On the other hand, if you tell the same children that you have full confidence in their ability to perform the task, the chances are very good that they will do it even if it means stretching their abilities—again, individually, there will be exceptions.

How does all of the foregoing apply to this discussion? In the next few paragraphs, I am going to describe a fairly common condition facing most housewives, particularly the wives of professional men and executives. The particular reaction that any one person makes to those conditions will be dependent on her own personal makeup (individual differences). To all of the general statements I make there will be *exceptions*. And, the extent to which any one person will attempt to overcome her own problems will depend upon how important it is to her to achieve a more satisfying existence and thus greater personal happiness (motivation).

THE PROBLEM

The best expression I can offer of the problem facing most
housewives is found in the five-act play located in Chapter 3
of this book. The major points contained in that play are as
follows:

1. A young couple—usually he is a college graduate, though
that need not be—begin life together with common interests
and work together in almost everything they do.

2. He slowly begins to get wrapped up in his career, and she
finds herself increasingly absorbed in the problems of raising children and taking care of the house.

3. They arrive at middle age:

He: Has continued to grow intellectually and as a
person.

She: Knows all about diapers, baby food, and housework, but little else.

4. Problem: They have grown apart and now find themselves
with very little in common—nothing, really, to hold their
marriage together. In effect, she has become a detriment to
him and, in a very real sense, to herself.

Many people might consider these conditions as somewhat
extreme. However, the five-act play and the summary listed
above were derived not out of my imagination but rather
from a common story told to me again and again and again by
people who have lived the experience.

In one sense, this statement of the problem does a major
injustice to what is really a very complicated set of problems.

• Because of the varied tasks they must perform, a husband
and wife (where the wife stays home to raise the family) are
going to experience a divergence of life styles. Each will have
different demands to face and different kinds of problems to
cope with.

• The wife will be forced to make concessions to her husband's career, especially if he is in a profession or, in the business world, striving for promotion to executive position. Very likely, he will have to travel a great deal, and she must stay home alone with the children. He will work long hours and expect her to adapt to them, since it is his activities that must take precedence where a conflict occurs.

• As time goes on she will have more and more time available (as the children become more self sufficient), whereas he will experience the narrowing effect of an ever-increasing demand for professional competence on a constantly current basis.

• And so on. Each type of problem requires a special answer. Here, our concern is solely with what she can do to avoid the Mid-Life Crisis—in this instance the very special expression of that crisis in the separation and alienation that happen so frequently to young couples who do not make a deliberate attempt to avoid it.

THE SOLUTION

The solution to avoid the Mid-Life Crisis in the first place, or to cope with it when it does occur is exactly the same. The only difference is that it is easier to act in a preventive mode than it is to unravel a problem and then build constructively. Nevertheless, it can be done.

The solution is to become a more broadly gauged person, realize your latent talents and abilities, and become as much as possible of what you are capable of being.

(Note: In defining the methodology of the solution, I will take the approach of talking to the bride who wants to prevent the problem in the first place. HOWEVER, the middle-aged housewife—even one facing the reality of the problem—can follow the same program with minor modification and achieve a positive result.)

If you detect a certain similarity between the several steps suggested below and the 10 steps contained in Chapter 5 of this book, go to the head of the class. The basic concepts are the same, only the specific actions vary.

1. Recognize the Potential Problem. Anything I say on this point will be redundant. You must recognize the need, or you will not have the motivation to make the required effort to do what must be done. At the same time, you should recognize that very little can be accomplished quickly. What you are getting into is a long-term program that, if started at the beginning of your marriage, can proceed leisurely, as long as it moves steadily.

2. Begin the Process of Finding Out Who You Are. Even at this early date you should have some idea of your interests, aptitudes, and abilities. But you can expect these to change over time. Thus taking an inventory now and updating that inventory periodically is a good practice.

3. Incidentally, Keep Physically Fit with regular medical checkups and proper exercise. This is probably as good a place as any to attack and overcome one "cop-out" as an example of all the others. For almost *everything* that people *should* do, there are ten million "good reasons" why it can't be done. For example, most women claim they can't get any exercise because they (1) can't get to a gymnasium, (2) don't have time to leave their chores, (3) don't have the proper equipment, (4) etc., etc., etc. Any good library will supply a book on exercises that can be done at home—I even saw one a while ago that turned most household tasks into exercises that could be done simultaneously with the task. At the very least, you could find a spot that won't shake the house apart and run in place for 20 minutes three or four times a day.

The important point here is that every one of the suggestions I make throughout this book can be done—*IF YOU REALLY WANT TO DO THEM.* You will probably have to adapt each to your own life and life style (individual differences) and perhaps take into account some specific set of circumstances (condition, physical disability, or other limitation) (exception), but you can do every one if you want to (motivation).

4. Stay in Tune with Your Husband's Career. Start at the very beginning to learn what your husband does for a living and stay with it as his career develops and his responsibilities grow. It is amazing how many women do not know what their husbands do for a living, other than in the most vague general terms. By making it your business to keep current with his job, you create a common point of interest that will serve as one excellent foundation for your marriage.

It is also very likely that some portion of your actual or potential social life will revolve around your husband's career. If you are not "in," you will be left out.

5. Read. The point of this suggestion is to be "informed" not just aware of what's going on. Thus your reading should get far beyond the newspaper headlines (or television headlines, which is all they are anyway) to include books, magazines, and anything else that's important.

Basically, I suggest that you attempt to be well informed in three areas:

a. First, read as much as you can that is relevant to your husband's career. This does not mean that you have to become as technically competent as he is. But, you should know—broadly—the important aspects of the things that affect him and what he does.

b. Second, you should know what's going on in the world. Today this is a very easy task. In addition to radio, television, and newspapers, there are several excellent news magazines (such as *Time*) that will help you stay in touch with what is going on in the world.

c. Finally, you have interests of your own. Between economical paperback books and public libraries, you will be hard-pressed to find a legitimate reason for not pursuing some interest.

6. Go to School. I recognize that school is not for everyone, or at least not for everyone to the same degree. On the other hand, there are an ever-growing variety of schools, offering courses on all sorts of topics. Even with small children on your hands, you can work out a way to learn anything from sewing to clothing design to chemical engineering—if you really want to. Some colleges have nurseries for student mothers (or mothers who are students, if you prefer it that way). The gal to whom this book is dedicated completed her bachelor's degree after our three children were in school. The graduation ceremony was a family affair.

7. Get Involved in Doing Something. Shop around. There is an endless variety of things you can do, ranging from personal hobbies to working in an organization. Try as many as you like—don't get trapped into something that you dislike or find disinteresting or from which you receive no satisfaction. The point of all this is to develop your abilities and to grow as a human being into as much as possible of what you are capable of being.

The other side of the coin should also be watched. Don't become an organizational butterfly, flitting from one thing to another without ever settling on something. Find the happy medium between the two and select that thing or those things that will enable you to make a contribution, provide you with an opportunity for your own personal growth, and, most important of all, give you an individual identity in your own right.

8. Don't Neglect Your Primary Job in the Home. With all that I have said about moving outside of the home, it is important to recognize that being an effective wife and mother is just as important, in its own right, as is anything else you can ever do. The point of all of the foregoing suggestions is to prepare for that time when your role will change—so that you will not be left behind, even though you did an excellent or even an outstanding job at what you are doing.

The most important point of all, here, is to look beyond what you are doing at any one point in time, plan for what can or will be, and thus avoid a problem rather than have to solve one. Avoiding problems is always easier, less painful, and more fun than solving them after they occur. Planning is usually the difference between avoidance and repair.

HOW TO COPE WITH A CRISIS YOU HAVEN'T AVOIDED

All of the foregoing refers to a basic plan aimed at avoiding a Mid-Life Crisis of the peculiar sort to which the wives of executives and professional men are most susceptible. Let me hasten to add that such problems are not the exclusive province of those groups, however, because exactly the same effect happens in families where the breadwinner (male) is not an executive or professional person, if the two people involved permit themselves to drift into the traps I have described.

Let's assume that, for whatever reason, you wake up one morning and come to the realization that you have a Mid-Life Crisis. You may recognize this by your awareness of the fact that your and your husband's lives have gone in different directions, to the point that you now have little in common that is real and substantive. Or, you may discover what you've known, but have been unwilling to accept, for a long time, that your life is basically unhappy. Or, upon some serious reflection, you may conclude that (for whatever reason) your life is essentially empty.

What can you do under these conditions?

Once again, the *correct* answer in your specific case cannot be prescribed here. To think that it could be is rank foolishness. On the other hand, there is a great deal you can do to help yourself find the answer.

As one approach, I would suggest the following:

1. Before anything else, it is necessary that you "sort out" the situation. This is necessary so that you can begin to gain some perspective on a problem in which you are a leading figure. Also, somewhere along the line you are going to have to work with someone else, and your ability to get help will be increased if you can describe the situation clearly and in a balanced fashion. I recognize that this process is extremely difficult, because your emotions and your ego defenses are going to be all intermingled with the facts. But, however difficult it may be and however inadequate the final product of your thinking, you will be better off than if you just run pell-mell to someone, for help, when you first recognize the problem. Once again, putting your thoughts in writing will help you sort things out faster than by trying to do it all in your head.

2. The next step, once you have analyzed the problem as thoroughly as you can by ourself, is to discuss it with someone else who can help you clarify the situation even further. Here, you have a number of options:

A. The *best* person to talk to, by far, is your husband, since it is his problem too and since he is also a major ingredient in the situation. Somewhere along the line you are going to have to talk to him. It is your relationship with him that is at the root cause of the problem or certainly a major contributing cause to the problem. It is quite likely that this conversation (even broaching it) will be difficult. However, it is worth the effort.

B. If, for whatever reason, you are unable to talk with your husband, the next best person might be your clergyman. If he is competent in these matters, he can be of real help not only in assisting you in defining the problem, but also in helping to develop a solution. It is entirely possible that, under the right conditions, he can work as a counselor with both you and your husband. However, if he is incompetent in these matters, it is best to avoid him.

C. A third choice of someone to talk to is a good friend. In this choice you must recognize that there is real potential danger. Since you are going to be talking about matters that are highly personal and intimate, you do not want someone who is merely an acquaintance, incapable of keeping a confidence, or likely to become emotionally involved. *You don't need sympathy.* What you need is *help.* Accordingly, it is extremely important that if you decide to talk to a friend that you be as sure as you possibly can that she or he is the "right" person in the first place.

D. If all else fails, one of your best sources of help is that of a professional counselor such as a psychologist or psychiatrist.

3. Once you have a good grasp on the situation, if you have not already done so, the next person to talk to is your husband, with whom you can work out the rest of the problem.
4. Finally, the specific things to do will be suggested by your analysis of the problem.

• Very likely, one of the first and foremost things you will have to do is to establish a channel of communication with your husband and embark on a process of building your relationship in that quarter on a sound basis.

• In addition, all the things suggested in Chapter 5 and in the foregoing part of this chapter are suggested as possible parts of your program.

Finally, I cannot and will not delude you by suggesting that what I propose (here or in any other part of this book) is simple or easy to accomplish. Nothing in life that is worthwhile is. On the other hand, most of the steps that I suggest are easier than they appear to be at first glance, but in the final analysis, whatever the effort, I *can* promise you that the result will be worth it.

8 Note to Pre-Middle-Agers —Prevention

The basic focus of this book has been on the definition, causes, and means for *overcoming* the Mid-Life Crisis.

As I have talked to individuals and groups on this topic, I have been asked, repeatedly, "How about those people who are not yet middle-aged—how can they avoid a Mid-Life Crisis?".

The answer to the question seems to me to be so clear that I usually try to find out whether there isn't something behind the question, and even after determining that there isn't, I am still not sure.

Because the question arises so often, however, the short remainder of this book is devoted to my answer.

BASIC FACT OF LIFE

Youth has great difficulty seeing the reality of middle age. Because they have known nothing (all their lives) other than physical and mental *growth and development,* a leveling off or deterioration in the process is almost unimaginable. In fact, for most people, until some personal experience of a traumatic sort occurs, there is no way that they can really understand or appreciate what the aging process is all about.

On the other hand, there is one matter of sufficient significance that should be recognized and on which work should be begun long before middle age becomes even a remote possibility. This is even more important when one recognizes that what I am going to suggest requires a great deal of time to bring to fruition and because:

- Doing it can well help one to avoid a Mid-Life Crisis.
- Once a crisis has occurred, there will be no time to do it.

What I am talking about here is the development of a *personal identity,* but I am talking about this concept as it really is, not as it is too often thought of today.

Your task is to develop an *internal* personal identity, one that enables you to think of yourself as having value—value independent of material values.

Most people depend on *external* values for their identity, and when these are removed they are left with nothing to fall back on. For example, if you were to ask the average executive, "Who are you?" the answers you would get would most likely be very similar and of the following variety:

- "I am John Jones, Vice President of Marketing for the XYZ Company."

If John Jones centers his personal identity on his role as a Vice President of the XYZ Company—as his *major* source of identification—once he retires he will have nothing left. This is a common condition, today, for retired people.

- For women it is less of a problem, where they can retain their identity as wife and mother.
- In the old days, it was not a problem, because usually people didn't retire or if they did, for whatever reason, they were still regarded as the person they had been, the mayor, the cobbler, the farmer, and so on.

There are several major points relevant to the concept of personal identity. Without attempting to put them in order of importance or relevance, they are merely listed below.

1. A large number (not a majority) of young people—teenagers and those in their early 20s—unable to face the challenge of growing up and unable to assume the responsibilities of becoming adults, drop out to "find themselves." This dropping out may take the form of a long vacation as a parasite on "old Dad," relatives, or society in general. Or it may be that the emotionally disturbed child may "play" at going to college, "play" at working and/or merely "play" at living. Let me assure you, this is not an attempt to establish a personal identity, even though it does in some cases, signify a need for professional help.

2. The need for a personal identity is twofold. First it is necessary, if a person is to achieve happiness, that he know who he is on a fairly realistic basis. (Walter Mitty enjoyed his daydreams, but he was constantly at odds with the world and outside of his fantasies was quite unhappy.) Beyond that point, however, knowing who you are enables you to integrate all facets of your life and serves as one of the elements that helps you to keep the various parts in balance, even when there are major changes in your circumstances.

3. Early in his existence on this earth, man found himself with several problems he couldn't handle—by himself.

• Where did he come from?

• What is life or the life force? (A dead body has everything that a live body has except "life.")

• What is at the end of space?

• How can man's mastery over the earth be reconciled with the totally incomprehensible powers of nature, and with his (man's) own infinite fragility and tenuous grip on life?

• On what can he base a good self-image (essential to happiness and good mental health), considering his knowledge of the facts that on both ends of his life he did and will live helplessly dependent on others, he cannot stop or even slow the aging process, and (worst of all) eventually he must die?

Based on these and many more mysteries, man developed the concept of the soul (invisible), the concept of God (invisible and all-powerful, even though any Jew or Christian worthy of the name knows that God exists independent of man or man's inventive genius), escapism (through fantasy) and many others. The values emanating from these concepts enable men to live together in society. On the other hand, when man is weak, human, and fallible, he derogates his own values. That is, he tries to control God through (1) prayer, (2) collective and individual bargaining, and (3) by reducing God to his—man's—level of comprehension. The problem here is that the rejection which occurs often includes the bathwater and the baby—man's imperfect exercise of his values causes him to reject those values, without providing a suitable substitute, even though the basic problems still exist.

Many young people today deride the values of the older generation, without recognizing the basis for those values and also without recognizing that those same values, no matter how poorly expressed, serve as a basis for the identity of the people whom they put down. It is this fact that has helped to fuel the fires of the generation gap and has caused guilt feelings among many middle-agers, who recognize the feelings, but don't know what they feel guilty about.

4. One of the most common ways in which people learn is through imitation. At the same time, as noted in the preceding point, since the beginning of his existence, man has developed something outside of himself to explain the incomprehensible mysteries of the universe. As another facet in this same process, man needs heroes to emulate. It doesn't really matter whether the person so chosen indeed has the values ascribed to him. What matters is that the hero worshipper believes he does and attempts to model himself after the hero figure.

Today, too many young people reject the heroes of their parents—heroes who are believed to be patriots, honest, dedicated to the positive development of society and otherwise outstanding examples of old fashioned virtues. One might say, "So what?" The answer is simply that too often in an attempt at family harmony, the parents will reject the hero and in some cases even adopt the hero of the child. The rejection of these heroes is bad enough by itself, but the matter is made a matter of real concern when one examines the heroes that these same young people have chosen for themselves—people, by and large, who have made no contribution of any sort to society, people whose lives exemplify (in too many cases) some of the worst things that man can be and, frequently, people who glorify the improper use of drugs and alcohol. (That may sound very prudish, and it does. But while you think that—go take a look at a drunk who is beating up on his 3-year-old child because the baby is crying and he feels mean, or at a 16-year-old hooker who is feeding both a pimp and a *habit*.)

Finally, putting everything I have said in this section together, three points—in summary—are of vital importance:

• First, the development of a personal identity will go a long way to eliminate the occurrence of many Mid-Life Crises and will facilitate the overcoming of others.

• Developing a meaningful personal identity takes a great deal of time and should begin long before the person starts to even think about becoming middle-aged.

• In the process of developing a personal identity, it is important to recognize that adherence to many of the values, beliefs, and philosophies of your peers may divert you from achieving your purpose. Thus doing what is best for yourself may (and probably will) require that you think for yourself and develop sufficient intestinal fortitude to control your own life rather than dumbly hand it over to others whose primary interests are their own and not yours.

NECESSARY CONDITION

Before the pre-middle-age person will be willing to do something constructive about his own future middle age, he must be convinced that such an event will actually occur in his life. To be truly effective, such a realization should not be viewed morbidly as something to be dreaded. Rather, as I have stressed elsewhere in this book, the desirable condition is to see life as a continuous stream of growth and evolution, with each stage along the way different from, but as good as every other.

If the pre-middle-age person can achieve a properly constructive and positive view of his whole life, then all of my advice is tied up in the 10 steps in Chapter 5 of this book. The same suggestions will apply to those who want to avoid a Mid-Life Crisis, just as it does to those who are already experiencing such a problem. In fact, having time and without the pressure of an existing crisis situation, avoiding the problem will be a great deal easier than trying to solve it after it happens.

With the necessary commitment and effort, the Mid-Life Crisis need never occur. It is all up to you!

Index